MADE IN ALBERTA:

The Ray Martin Story

By
Ray Martin and John Ashton
Introduction by
Hon. Rachel Notley, MLA

Made in Alberta: The Ray Martin Story Copyright © 2018 by Ray Martin and John Ashton. All Rights Reserved.

All rights reserved. No part of this book may be reproduced in any form or by any electronic or mechanical means including information storage and retrieval systems, without permission in writing from the author. The only exception is by a reviewer, who may quote short excerpts in a review.

Cover designed by John Ashton and Olav Rokne Cover photographs by Olav Rokne

Author Name
Visit my website at www.AuthorName.com

Printed in the United States of America

First Printing: Aug 2017
Name of Company

ISBN-9781720017073

Acknowledgements

Ray and John would like to thank David Herbert for his research assistance, Geoff Geddes for acting as editor, and Olav Rokne for his cover photography.

Ray's Dedication

"I would like to dedicate this book to my family whose support has been crucial on my journey in pursuing my progressive agenda; attempting to build a better and fairer society. I was especially influenced by two strong women who have since passed away. I am, of course, talking about my mother, Olive, and my wife, Cheryl Matheson."

"From my past, I include, Grant Notley who was my mentor and good friend. He was my Best Man in my marriage to Cheryl. I still think of him often."

"I would also like to dedicate this book to countless New Democrats in the Province and Country whose time and effort made the success I had in the political work a possibility".

"I am very fortunate to have my wife, Evelyn David, by my side. Besides the emotional support she provides every day, she has been very helpful in reviewing the content of this book."

"Finally, a big thank you to John Ashton who persevered over a long period of time to bring this book to its conclusion. This has been a difficult challenge and I am grateful." – Ray

John's Dedication

John would like to thank his parents for telling him that he could do this. He would also like to thank all the people who said "yes" when they were asked to support Ray over forty years.

MADE IN ALBERTA: The Ray Martin Story

Introduction

By Hon. Rachel Notley, MLA

On October 18th, 1984, during an evening sitting of the legislature, my dad rose and gave what would end up being his final full address to the Chamber. Ray Martin sat at his side – the 'caucus' in the Alberta NDP's first ever Official Opposition.

Dad quoted the Pope, who had recently finished a tour of Canada, speaking powerfully to Canadians about "the primacy of people over things." Dad seized on that line and said, "growing numbers of Canadians and Albertans are beginning to ask whether or not, in making decisions, it isn't time to restore people to the primacy..." Dad spoke about a social policy regime in shambles that failed people. As evidence, he told the story of the tragic death of a young Indigenous man in foster care, Richard Cardinal. One member of the government caucus heckled, "where were his parents?" and I can only imagine the stony stare that un-named MLA would have received from my dad and Ray. He spoke of the programs of the day and their failure to address the barriers faced by women in the workforce. He ended his comments by moving that the legislature recognize the government's failure to consider "the major role of women in the Alberta economy or the unique problems currently faced by women in their attempts to secure greater participation in our provincial economy."

Shortly after, Ray rose, and with his characteristically dry wit, said, "It may come as a shock to people, but I'm going to rise and support the amendment."

The primacy of everyday people and the need to put the wellbeing of average Albertans first has always been the soil in which New Democrats are rooted. Those roots are what Ray tended and defended for decades, keeping the NDP alive through a lot of rainless seasons. It should come as no surprise that someone as down to earth as Ray would be the one to oversee our roots, and it is no stretch to say our win in 2015 wouldn't have happened were it not for Ray Martin.

Ray became a truly close friend of my father's in the 70s. Dad often had to spend 5-6 days a week in Edmonton. Refusing to pay for a 'nice' hotel, or for dinner, Dad would instead hang out at Ray's house, along with Ray's wife Cheryl. They would spend many nights plotting the future of the party and their friendship grew.

The very first time Ray got elected, in 1982, he joined with my dad to become Alberta's Official Opposition. I was working as a nanny in

MADE IN ALBERTA: The Ray Martin Story

France, so I wasn't there when this two-person landmark was achieved by our party. When I returned in 1983, dad was Leader of the Official Opposition and the first thing he did was drive me to the legislature to show off the new suite of offices he and Ray had earned. Given it was just the two of them, it was tempting to tease them and ask, "That's it?" But to see how proud he and Ray were, and how much Albertans respected them, standing up to the Tory machine, two against the rest - it was an image of them I will remember.

From the day of my dad's death in October of 1984, and for a long time afterwards, Ray's fight to lead the party's recovery from the loss of dad paralleled our family's effort to recover from the loss of a father and husband. The two efforts were intertwined and so it will come as no surprise that the election of May 1986 was special. Ray led the party to its most successful result in the party's history to that point – electing sixteen New Democrats to Alberta's legislature, in a campaign that focused on the wellbeing of everyday people. After the tragedy of Dad's death, the celebration that election night brought New Democrats in Alberta together in a way about which many families in mourning can only dream.

Ray and the team held those seats in 1989, but in 1993, when faced with a neo-conservative campaign initiated by the Liberals and embraced by the PCs, the NDP lost all sixteen seats, including Ray's. It was then, ironically, that Ray's true dedication and loyalty to our movement came to the fore. Ray would run again – a lot. He ran to be a school trustee, to be an MLA, to be an MP. Sometimes he won, sometimes he lost, but he never forgot why he was there, the change he was seeking to make, and the good he was trying to accomplish for people.

There are many stories about Ray's campaigns. But perhaps the one that resonates with me the most is his decision to run in Edmonton-Glenora in 2012. Months before his decision to run in that race, in 2011, Ray had come frustratingly close to being elected in Jack Layton's orange wave. Even more importantly he was faced with the tragic loss of his beloved wife Cheryl only weeks later. Yet, soon after Cheryl's death, he agreed to help me in the job of recruiting candidates for the upcoming provincial election. Perhaps it was a way to help him emerge from his grief, but Ray was good at recruiting people and very successful. But one area remained a challenge – Edmonton-Glenora. We had almost won this older neighbourhood, just west of downtown, in 2004. But we were having a terrible time convincing someone the party had a chance in this area that was traditionally seen as very wealthy. Then, in a meeting with Brian Mason and me, Ray dropped a bomb: He wanted to be the NDP candidate there.

As surprised as I was to hear Ray say that, it made sense to me. Ray was a recognized personality across the city, and voters had proven themselves open to supporting the NDP in those neighbourhoods where Ray had stood for office. I said to Ray, "You'll show the world that we can win Edmonton-Glenora, even if we don't win Edmonton-Glenora." Up to 2015, the way you won a seat in Alberta if you were a New Democrat was to start by coming in a close second. That's exactly what Ray did, raising money and recruiting volunteers in the process. And then he kept at it. As we approached 2015, the groundwork he'd laid helped recruit Sarah Hoffman as a candidate in that riding. She won, and I like to think she is the best Minister of Health the province has seen in decades, if ever. Ray made it happen.

This specific story doesn't describe the many successes Ray achieved personally. But building the NDP in Alberta over the last fifty years has never been about overnight success. It has been a determined commitment to the many years of work it takes to scratch out electoral success. It is that tenacity that positioned our party to win government in 2015, while so many political watchers were looking the other way, and it is that tenacity that defines Ray Martin's life long commitment to our movement.

The electoral success of 2015 is due in large part to Ray's work, in the face of all his challenges, wins, and defeats. Long after he stepped down as leader, he kept on as a hard-working fighter for the people conservatives so often forget. After the personal loss he endured in 1993 or even 2008, ninety-nine out of a hundred politicians would have walked away from public life. But Ray was that one in a hundred, and he showed himself to be far more dedicated than just anyone.

Looking back, it is no surprise dad and Ray became quick, close friends. In the 1970's, dad could be shy and awkward, but if you dug a little deeper, he was really funny. Ray, on the other hand, was outgoing, extroverted, and always fun. I think dad gravitated to Ray because of how at ease Ray has always been in his own skin, that and a stoicism dad recognized in Ray that is a form of prairie resilience. There's a way Ray has, one that anyone growing up on, or near, a farm will recognize; his understated drawl, his ability to laugh off whatever the world throws at him, and, ultimately his ability to stick it out, no matter the circumstances. You see that stoic resilience in farming communities like the one Ray grew up in and in rural communities across Alberta. It's a resilience born during drought years or heavy rain years, when the crops don't come in and families at the post office put on their bravest faces, crack jokes, and remain firm in the knowledge they've done whatever they could in the face of elements beyond their control. It is a resilience born from a commitment to those values so clearly shared by dad and Ray through the NDP. Ray knew he was there to stand up for regular Albertans, for Albertans who did not otherwise have a voice, and for Albertans whose voice was just not being heard. That principled approach drove how he practiced politics for more than 40 years.

And so, we are a better province because of Ray Martin.

Ray's Elections

Year	Position	Where	Result
1975	Member of the Legislative Assembly	Calgary McKnight	2nd, 13.8%
1979	Member of the Legislative Assembly	Edmonton Norwood	2nd, 38.1%
1982	**Member of the Legislative Assembly**	**Edmonton Norwood**	**1st, 46.2%**
1986	**Member of the Legislative Assembly**	**Edmonton Norwood**	**1st, 69.2%**
1989	**Member of the Legislative Assembly**	**Edmonton Norwood**	**1st, 57.6%**
1993	Member of the Legislative Assembly	Edmonton Norwood	2nd, 32.4%
1997	Member of Parliament	Edmonton North	3rd, 14.9%
2000	Member of Parliament	Edmonton Centre-East	3rd, 17.4%
2001	**Edmonton Public School Board Trustee**	**Ward D**	**1st, 66.3%**
2004	**Member of the Legislative Assembly**	**Edmonton Beverly-Clareview**	**1st, 50.8%**
2008	Member of the Legislative Assembly	Edmonton Beverly-Clareview	2nd, 36.4%
2008	Member of Parliament	Edmonton East	2nd, 31.8%
2011	Member of Parliament	Edmonton East	2nd, 37.4%
2012	Member of the Legislative Assembly	Edmonton Glenora	2nd, 25.6%
2013	**Edmonton Public School Board Trustee**	**Ward D**	**1st, 60.8%**

Elections as Alberta NDP Leader

Year	Position	Votes	% of Vote	Seats
1986	Leader of the Opposition	208,561	29.2%	16
1989	Leader of the Opposition	217,972	26.3%	16
1993	3rd	108,883	11.0%	0

Part 1: Roots

I've never really looked into my family tree. You see ads on TV telling you about websites and services that will do it for you, but you always think you'll get to it later.

On my father's side of the family, the only grandparent I really knew well was my paternal grandfather, John Martin. He was a crusty old Scotsman, who immigrated from the Isle of Lewis, north of Scotland. It's a godforsaken rocky island, and it's no surprise that Alberta looked a lot better to my grandfather.

After serving in the Boer War, John came to Alberta and was a farming pioneer in the Delia area. He would retire to Vancouver in British Columbia before I was born, but he visited us often.

He was quite a character. He would occasionally slip me $20 on the sly. That was quite a lot of money for a kid in those days. Years later, he was celebrated as the last living veteran of the Boer War.

I know even less about my mother's roots. I never met her parents. She had lived in all four western provinces before marrying my father. And, in 1941, I came along.

I had a great childhood. It wasn't perfect, but I have nothing but great memories of growing up in Delia. It's a small farming town, a two-hour drive east of Calgary, close to Drumheller and Hanna. It was a tight-knit community that kids don't experience today, so I felt lucky. Anyone could be from Edmonton, or another big city, but I get to be from Delia.

Driving to Delia was beautiful. In my day, you'd see the grain elevators as you approach, and the Hand Hills in the background.

Delia gave me a childhood filled with friends, sports, and great experiences. It also laid the foundation for the values that would guide me through 45 years of political activism.

My earliest clear memory is meeting my father, Jim Martin, for the first time when I was four years old. We were standing at the Calgary train station and my mother was kissing a strange man. He turned out to be my dad.

He had served four years as a sergeant in World War II, stationed in Europe without a single break. In my opinion, he came back from that experience pretty screwed up, probably with post-traumatic stress syndrome.

Today, we know a lot more about what happens to people coming home from war. We saw the struggle that Canadian troops went through when they returned from Afghanistan. We at least understand something of that struggle and try to help where we can.

This wasn't the case in my father's day. He dealt with his experience with silence and alcohol. While he certainly wasn't abusive, he was distant and often absent. He did maintain the family farm, which provided some of our household income.

He preferred to spend his free time at the Delia hotel bar, until it burnt down. After that, he would visit pubs in neighbouring towns. The drinking put a serious strain on our relationship.

In my adult years, I came to better understand what my father had gone through. While he never revealed much of his war experience, we did reconcile. Eventually, we got to a point where we could talk and socialize.

Unfortunately, my dad's struggles left my mother, Olive, to raise me pretty much single-handedly. She did this along with running her own insurance business and working for the village of Delia as secretary-treasurer. In the process, she instilled the values that I carried with me into politics.

My mother ran her life and her office as a progressive. She believed in sticking up for the little person. She believed in the necessity of unions. She believed in equality.

For example, the Municipality of Delia ran programs for new mothers and infant children for the village. There was one unwed mother who attended. In 1950s small town Alberta, that was not a popular position to be in. But my mother always made a point of fussing over her child first, sending the message that this woman deserved equal treatment.

That being said, mom still supported the right-wing Social Credit Party. The Co-operative Commonwealth Federation, the forerunner party to the New Democratic Party, had no presence in Delia. In fact, there were no provincial CCF candidates that ran in Hand Hills (the district name) from 1948 to 1959.

I had no brothers or sisters growing up, but I was hardly isolated. There were always other kids in our home, and vice versa. My closest childhood friend, Bill Sloan, practically lived in my home at times.

For my first year in school, we still lived on the farm. I attended first grade in a one-room schoolhouse called Newport School. We then moved into Delia, and I started Grade One in the local school, where I remained right through to high school graduation.

I was a bit of a lazy student. I gave enough effort to pass, but not much more, unless it was a subject that interested me. I usually was well-behaved and got along with teachers, but still got strapped occasionally.

I was much more interested in sports. Almost every moment that I wasn't at school or working odd jobs and my paper route, I was playing sports.

Like any Alberta boy, hockey was my favourite. I played with a number of teams over the years, including ones for Delia and Hanna. I played forward and I was pretty good, but not necessarily the best on the team.

In those days, there were no helmets. Shoulder pads were seldom seen. I didn't play on artificial ice until I was 14. I was never injured, and I suspect this is largely due to the game being slower than it is today. There was the odd fight, and I admittedly started a few, (to the embarrassment of my mother). I did lose some teeth over time, and to this day I have a partial plate as a souvenir.

Our area didn't churn out any great hockey stars in my day. I did play against Lorne MacDonald, the father of Calgary Flames' star Lanny MacDonald, who was a real mean cuss. I got an offer for a tryout with the Moose Jaw Canucks., a Saskatchewan-based junior "A" team, but I passed on it, without regret. I just knew I wasn't the best player around.

Instead of a playing career, I got something much better: my start in coaching. I was given a chance to coach younger kids in hockey in Hanna. It was a wonderful experience, and I learned lessons that would serve me well in my teaching career.

There were other sports as well. As an older child, I was an enthusiastic curler, while baseball was my summer sport. Later in high school, I would play football for one season, and was a regional all-star in basketball.

By the time I reached high school, there were other diversions beyond sports. I was into 1950s pop culture as much as anyone. I liked James Dean movies. I listened to rock 'n' roll records from Elvis Presley (I copied his "duck-bill" haircut for a time), Bill Haley and Buddy Holly. I even went to Calgary to see the Everly Brothers. Every Thursday was movie night at the Legion Hall, something we never missed.

There would be plenty of gang fighting, mostly divided between towns. I'm not proud to say I was a willing participant.

We were most often clashing with the gritty Drumheller kids. Drumheller is more a tourist town now. In my childhood, it was a tough mining town full of tougher people. I even took a set of "knuckledusters", (also known as brass knuckles) from a Drumheller kid on one occasion.

As high school ended, I had decided that I wanted to teach physical education. Sports and coaching were my life at this point, so it wasn't hard to choose.

Delia is still a special place to me. When I served as leader of the Alberta NDP, we always made a stop during election tours. I still have friends there, and I visit often, but at the time, I wasn't broken up about leaving. It was the right time to move on.

Getting into university to become a qualified teacher wasn't going to be easy. I had to write six "departmental exams" or tests that were required to graduate. Though I scored 80% on three of my tests, the other three were in the 40% range. Clearly, I'd have to do some make-up courses before university.

Due to my three bad departmental exams, university was going to have to wait a year. So, for the fall, I went to work for a private surveyor firm. We did work for the provincial government, and I was employed as a chainman for road surveys and construction. That winter, I went to a high school in Red Deer to make up my three exams. Afterwards, I was hired by the Alberta Department of Highways, working on roads around the province.

It was while working on a road crew when I got another dose of left-wing political education. One of my co-workers was constantly complaining that private firms, like Calgary Power, were making big bucks off of taxpayers' money instead of the government performing this work in-house. It's a notion that made a lot of sense to me then. And after decades of failure with Alberta's expensive experiment with privatization and deregulation, it makes even more sense to me now.

Part 2: Education

The following September, I enrolled in the University of Alberta's Department of Education. Moving to Edmonton had been hectic. There was only one other person I knew from Delia there, and I hadn't lived in a city before.

That's a big reason why I applied to become a member of a fraternity on campus. I was "rushed" into Kappa Sigma. That meant I started to get invited to their parties and activities and got a sponsor. Not everyone was accepted, but I wasn't nervous about the rituals or the vote that would decide if I got in.

Yes, I got hazed. Just before I arrived on the scene, the local Kappa Sigma chapter had received notice from their central headquarters that paddling was to be discontinued. However, being as I was among the mouthiest of the new recruits, they decided to save one more round of paddling for myself and another guy. The truth is, we probably earned it. And we had the sense of humour to handle it.

While the paddle would be retired after my round with it, we found some creative ways to give the other new recruits a hard time too. In fact, I wound up developing some inventive hazing rituals myself. There were also a lot of parties and binge drinking, although I never saw anyone passed out or doing any harm to themselves or others.

Fraternity hazing gets a lot of criticism and negative attention these days, and I suspect it's deserved. I certainly don't have a problem with how I was treated, but I acknowledge that times have changed. That sort of behaviour may simply be inappropriate now.

In the early 1960s, many Canadian university fraternities were competing to set the world record for pushing a bed. My fraternity clinched that record for a time by pushing a bed along Highway 2 from Calgary to Edmonton in just 20 hours. It captured a lot of media attention, especially when we passed through Red Deer and were met by a throng of cameras and spectators.

Fraternity life wasn't all partying either. There were also scheduled study hours and quiet time. Kappa Sigma at the U of A produced some fairly serious scholars.

My time in the fraternity was a valuable experience. It was my home for a year. It was my place to socialize in a town I didn't know, and it gave me friends that are part of my life to this day.

One of my fraternity brothers was Julian Koziak. Julian would go on to be an Alberta PC MLA and cabinet minister, and we served one term together in the Legislature from 1982 to 1986. He would lose his seat to NDP MLA Gordon Wright in our 1986 Edmonton sweep. Another frat brother was Harvie Andre, who would serve in Prime Minister Mulroney's PC government cabinet.

Sports still played a big part in my life. While I didn't regret passing on my tryout with the Moose Jaw Canucks, I do regret skipping tryouts for the University of Alberta Golden Bears hockey team. I think I could have made that team, but I'd gotten a bit lazy with hockey after missing a year. I played for the Education Faculty intramural team, as well as flag football.

To pay for school, I had accepted a large bursary from the County of Lacombe, south of Edmonton. In the 1960s, you could teach after two years of university, and I owed the County a year of teaching. I was assigned to teach Grade Six in Alix, Alberta. Alix was a farming town about two hours' drive south of Edmonton, and the majority of the students were from the farms, much like Delia.

I had a great time. It confirmed that the choice I'd made to become a teacher was the right one. It also made me take school a lot more seriously. In my first two years in university, I was still coasting academically. I would do enough to pass, and that was it. Alix taught me that a teaching career was worth working hard for.

I also had to spend a summer in the toughest job I ever had. I worked at a brutally hot steel mill in Edmonton's east end. We worked in short half-hour shifts moving red-hot steel rods off a conveyor belt with half-hour breaks to cool down. We even had to take salt pills to keep from dehydrating.

It was good money, but I saw what kind of working conditions people had to endure. One of my co-workers couldn't sweat anymore and had been told to quit. But he was an immigrant and couldn't have gotten that kind of income anywhere else.

A year later, my graduation was big news back home in Delia. My mother emphatically believed in the value of education and was extremely happy that I had a degree. Not many Delia folks had ever graduated from university. I was less impressed. I didn't even attend the ceremony.

Part 3: Calgary

When I graduated, my first – and only – teaching job application was to the Calgary Board of Education. Calgary was the place I wanted to be. The southern Alberta city was growing fast and would be the easiest place for me to get a job. It would also keep me close to my mother.

My first high school was Viscount Bennett in south Calgary. I started teaching physical education and social studies and was coaching various sports as well. The Viscount Bennett School building still exists today, as an adult learning centre.

I was a young, single teacher working with other young teachers. We partied a lot, especially with only other unmarried teacher there. We were nicknamed "The Piss Tank Twins" by the married teachers.

In 1967, I married my first wife, Ede, while I was at Viscount Bennett. We rented a house for a while, but soon moved into a home in the Huntington Hills suburb of north Calgary. She had a child from a first marriage, Bruce, who I quickly adopted. That seemed like a big leap to some, but it wasn't for me. In fact, it was an easy choice because Bruce was a great kid and was very easy to parent.

That same year, there was a provincial election. I got canvassed at home by none other than future PC Premier Peter Lougheed. I'm sure he didn't remember it, but I found him kind of impressive at the time; in fact, I may have even voted for him.

I watched that election closely. I also noticed the buzz surrounding then-Premier Ernest Manning and Garth Turcott. Turcott was an NDP MLA who had shocked the province in 1966 by winning a by-election in Pincher Creek-Crowsnest, a rural riding with lots of mines southwest of Calgary. Manning seemed to spend all his time in Turcott's riding. It was like he was fixated on having Turcott lose his seat and nothing else, and I found this annoying.

But I didn't take an active role in politics for the first time until 1968, and it wasn't with the New Democrats. That year, I got swept up in Trudeaumania, like so many others of my generation. I volunteered for Calgary South Liberal candidate Patrick Morgan Mahoney, who won narrowly.

On election night, I wasn't surprised to find the Liberal members celebrating, but I was surprised by *what* they were celebrating: the defeat of legendary NDP Leader Tommy Douglas in his own riding of Burnaby-

Seymour. They were as ecstatic at Douglas being kicked out of the House of Commons as they were at winning the first Liberal majority victory since 1953.

This didn't sit well with me. I was excited by Trudeau, but I thought Douglas to be a good man, and he had impressed me in the leaders' debates. That night soured me on the Liberal party, and I haven't thought any better of it since. Trudeau, circa 1968, was an empty canvas that a lot of people superimposed their own values over. This was certainly true in my case.

At the same time, I found that the same competitive nature that makes a good athlete also makes a good political activist. 45 years later, that still holds true.

Ede and I soon had a daughter, Dawn. In those days, fathers weren't in the room for the birth. So that night, I had to wait it out with some friends in a hospital waiting room on my birthday. Dawn was also a great kid and went on to be a fantastic college athlete.

I hadn't thought much about being a father prior to Bruce and Dawn coming into my life, but it was a huge reward watching them grow up to be fine adults.

Fatherhood isn't hard or easy, it's just a responsibility. It was a lot of work, but in truth, motherhood was much harder work for Ede.

In 1969, I decided to return to school. I was awarded a large bursary to get my Vocational Guidance Diploma in Education at the University of Calgary. My experience in coaching had pointed me toward switching to guidance counselling. Coaching teaches you about building a closer relationship with your students, which is a good trait for a guidance counsellor.

I spent a year doing the required classes and did a little substitute teaching on the side. I didn't coast through school this time either. I had a new family that I was responsible for. Between the bursary and the substitute teaching, I had more money that year than I made while teaching at Viscount Bennett. The summer were spent working on my thesis. I graduated with a Master of Science in Education Psychology.

I got my first guidance counsellor job at Bowness High School, northwest of Calgary, where I also coached basketball.

Bowness was a distinct community, but it has since gotten swallowed up by Calgary's urban sprawl, much like Beverly in Edmonton or Etobicoke in Toronto.

1971 brought another Alberta election. This one would prove to be historic for the province. I would get my second taste at political activism, and again, it wasn't with the NDP.

A close friend of mine, Calvin Lee (Cal for short), decided to run for the Progressive Conservatives. This was not the "safe" thing to do in 1971. Social Credit was still governing the province and had done so since 1935. The PCs only had ten seats going into that election and no one saw a PC government coming. Cal came to me, and other friends, to help his campaign.

By this point, I was already uncomfortable with small-c conservative ideals, regardless if it came with a Social Credit or Progressive Conservative label. But I'm loyal to my friends, so I agreed to help him win his nomination, and that would be the end of it.

So, for a short time, I was a member of the Progressive Conservative Party. I also helped to sign up other NDP friends to vote for Cal's nomination. If you were hoping to read something scandalous, there it is.

Cal won his nomination as the PC candidate for Calgary McKnight. I told Cal that his nomination campaign was as far as I could go with him. I couldn't stomach campaigning for the PC party.

Almost immediately afterward, I was signed up by Ralph Eng as an NDP member. As so often happens in the Alberta NDP, I was almost immediately asked to be a candidate in Calgary Foothills, along with my good friend Jim Staples. The two of us were pretty much all the NDP activists that this north Calgary riding had.

But I wasn't willing to be a candidate yet. It was the summer, and I hadn't taken that season off from work or study in some years. Now I had two children to spend it with, and Jim was of a similar mind. A coin-flip between Jim and I served as the NDP nomination meeting. I won the toss, and Jim became the "next NDP MLA for Calgary Foothills".

The election was held over the month of August. For Jim and I, our tiny campaign became our summer project, so we decided to have some fun with it.

For example, PC candidate Len Werry and Social Credit candidate Jay Salmon would set up fancy trailers in the parking lot of the local shopping mall at the corner of Brentwood and University. Jim and I certainly didn't have any trailers at our disposal, but we did have a pup tent. We set up that pup tent between the trailers and put our NDP sign out front. Our gag earned us a photo in the papers.

Neither of us had much time for door-to-door canvassing, but we were determined to get at least a few streets done. Anyone who has been around a successful election campaign will tell you that door-to-door canvassing is an absolute necessity if you're to have any chance of winning. Today, I start canvassing as early as two years before an election starts. In our tiny campaign, Jim and I were just hoping to get a couple of Saturdays in.

On a sunny Calgary afternoon, Jim and I set out to canvass a north Calgary suburban street. It wasn't easy. People were polite, but they weren't interested in voting for Jim or the NDP.

Jim knocked on the door of an especially crabby individual. He started screaming at Jim, accusing him of being a "communist bum". By this point, Jim had reached his boiling point, and gave the surly resident as good as he had gotten.

"You're the first son of a bitch I've met this election" is what Jim bellowed, loud enough for everyone on the block to hear. To say the least, yelling at any voter is breaking a cardinal rule of canvassing.

Jim stormed off that doorstop. Depressed, we debated whether or not to just give up and go get a beer.

"I'm not going to let that guy intimidate us," said Jim. "Let's at least finish the block."

We went to knock on the surly man's neighbouring door and introduced ourselves. Much to our surprise, he responded with "I've never voted NDP, but anyone willing to tell that son of a bitch off next door can have my vote."

This would become my favourite story to recount as a staffer travelling with the leader, as a candidate, and as a leader myself. In fact, if you've been an NDP member for any time, you've probably heard me tell it a dozen times or more.

Jim Staples didn't win Calgary-Foothills, garnering 9% of the vote. But it had all been a lot of fun. Len Werry won the riding, and my friend Cal Lee won his seat in Calgary-McKnight as well.

Three very important results came out of that election. I believe two of them irreversibly changed the province, and the third changed me forever.

The first is obvious. The Social Credit Party's 36-year-old government came to an end and was replaced by Peter Lougheed and the Progressive Conservative Party. Lougheed and the PCs were fresh young faces then and had managed to charm a more urban Alberta into giving them 49 out of 75 seats.

The second happened a long way from my home in Calgary. In Fairview, a town deep in northwestern Alberta, Grant Notley celebrated winning the NDP's only seat. After the CCF had lost their two seats in 1959, there had been no progressive voice in the Alberta Legislature since, apart from Garth Turcott's brief stay. But now there would be one voice, and a very loud one at that. I met Grant for the first time during that campaign and would get to know him better soon after that election.

You probably know about those two events. But you probably haven't heard about the third. BC NDP Leader David Barrett visited Calgary to support the NDP campaign. At his visit, Ede and I met another couple,

Barry Pashak and Cheryl Matheson. Cheryl would soon become a huge part of my life.

I switched into a new job in 1972. I became head of the Guidance Department at Ernest Manning High School in west Calgary on 17th Avenue. It meant being the boss of a group of guidance counsellors, and I found that I liked being a leader.

My days were filled with a lot of meetings, both at the school and at the Board office, and a large amount of student counselling. I also kept a hand in teaching by offering a careers course.

At the same time, I taught a self-hypnosis program. Don't let the term fool you; it's purely a tool for relaxation and stress reduction. I had been trained in the technique at the University of Calgary. As I said, Calgary was a different place in those days, and both students and parents were more open to new ideas. Shortly afterwards, hypnotism became associated with entertainment, magic acts, and so forth.

I continued coaching at Manning as well in junior basketball and wrestling. And that's where I got to meet members of one of Calgary's most famous families.

The Hart family has produced several famous professional wrestlers. Their children went to Manning High School, and I coached two of them in wrestling: Dean and Bret. Bret became better known as Bret "The Hitman" Hart, as a professional wrestler.

They were part of our successful wrestling team, which made it to the provincial championships. Bret won a medal at that tournament. In those days, I thought Bret and Dean were great kids and team members.

Later in the 1980s, as Bret became famous, the now-defunct *Alberta Report* magazine did an article about Bret's childhood in Calgary. They went through the high school yearbooks, found that the current Alberta NDP Leader (me) had been Bret's high school coach, and included that fact in the article. This in turn garnered attention from Calgary TV station CFCN and Bret wound up doing an interview which was broadcasted nationally. His father, Stu Hart (a wrestling legend in his own right) also told the Calgary Sun that he thought I had helped convince Bret to stay in school.

I certainly don't take credit for any of the prowess either of them showed in professional wrestling. I taught Dean and Bret a few things, but none of the WWF stuff. If I had a positive impact in their lives, I'm glad. It was certainly a positive experience for me being their coach.

That was the case with dozens of other students as well, regardless of what they achieved after my time with them. I still get a kick that I get asked about my experiences with Bret to this day by people who have no idea that I used to lead a political party.

1972 and 1974 brought federal elections, and I volunteered for the NDP in Calgary for both elections. For whatever reason, we focused more on the visits from our federal NDP Leader, David Lewis, as opposed to organizing local riding campaigns.

In 1972, we packed the Stampede Grounds, and I remember Lewis coming onstage and announcing "Here I am in Calgary. Do you think there's any welfare bums here?" That got quite a cheer.

He led a successful campaign denouncing the practice of giving profitable corporations subsidies and tax breaks at a cost to the citizens of Canada and their services. He came back in 1974 to another successful rally, and my daughter Dawn landed in the newspapers in a photo handing Lewis some flowers.

It was about that point that I decided to be a candidate myself for the first time. I chose Calgary-McKnight to run in, in spite of the fact it meant running against my friend, Cal Lee. The riding of Calgary McKnight was made up of north Calgary subdivisions, just west of the Deerfoot Trail.

Ed Broadbent came and spoke at my nomination a few months before he would become leader of the NDP. We amassed a respectable budget, but it wasn't enough for a full-time campaign manager. I quickly started door-knocking and found that the response was friendly, but Calgary was still enamoured with Lougheed.

We got a surprise. Cal Lee announced he wouldn't run again, in spite of only serving for one term. It certainly wasn't because he was afraid of running against me. Cal had found business opportunities he wanted to pursue, and he wound up settling in Sherwood Park. The PCs nominated Eric Musgrave to replace him.

When the election was called, we put together a pretty active campaign. My family worked hard on it. We had the funds to get billboards, leaflets, and signs, and had a good crew of volunteers, including my friend Cheryl Matheson. Grant Notley's tour did a great job covering the province, which helped us as well.

I came a respectable second with almost 14% and edged out the Social Credit candidate, which was considered impressive at the time. But Musgrave won easily. I didn't run into Eric very often. He would go on to serve as one of the PC's more moderate MLAs.

Provincially, Peter Lougheed had his foot on the neck of the Social Credit and reduced them to only four seats. Grant barely held onto his seat and there were no other New Democrats elected. The PCs won everything else.

Part 4: Organizer

After that election, I was completely hooked into political activism. I enjoyed being a candidate, and the fact that I didn't win didn't damper my enthusiasm.

There are a number of reasons why I was enthusiastic then, and still am now. It's gratifying to advocate for a set of values you philosophically believe in. It's also an amazing feeling to walk into a campaign office to see people volunteering and donating to support those same values.

The downside is that once you've been a candidate, all the other campaign jobs are boring by comparison. To this day, I'm still kind of bored in a campaign office if I'm not the name on the ballot.

Very shortly after election day, Grant Notley paid me a visit in Calgary to drop a proverbial bomb. He asked me to take on the job of provincial secretary of the Alberta NDP.

The provincial secretary (alternatively known as executive director) is an extremely crucial position in any political party, as it runs the day-to-day operations of the party office. That person is in charge of conventions, candidate searches, fundraising, election readiness, and tons of other responsibilities. Being offered this job came as a big surprise.

My first response was a "No." I loved working in education. It paid well, and my career was headed towards becoming a principal. The family was happy in Huntington Hills, and this job meant moving to Edmonton.

But I changed my mind just as quickly. As good as my life was, I was still addicted to politics and so was my wife. We saw the NDP as an even bigger cause than my education career. And I was flattered to be pursued by Notley and the party's executive.

I agreed to take on the job for one year. This was in spite of taking a 25% pay cut, or $6,000 (approximately $28,300 in 2018 dollars). The party's executive was happy to have me. The party's treasurer, Gordon Wright, responded to my hire with: "If he's crazy enough to take a $6,000 pay cut, let's get him right away."

I went to the Calgary School Board to negotiate an unpaid leave of absence. They were not thrilled about losing me for a year, and initially turned me down. I pointed out that I wouldn't be freeloading for the year, and I may have even threatened to quit altogether. They eventually relented and gave me the leave, so we packed up and moved to Edmonton.

My new workplace was a far cry from a nice, clean Calgary high school. It was on 97th street, just north of downtown Edmonton. The NDP office was where the Remand Centre jail now stands. It was a rough neighbourhood then, and still is. It was common to find people sleeping and fornicating around the building. But we made the best of it.

One of the first jobs was to pick a staff. I hired Lyle Bleich (pronounced *Bly*) as the party's bookkeeper and a young Ross Harvey as publisher of *The Democrat*, the party's newsletter. Beth Nielsen worked there as well.

My second job was to go to the 1975 federal NDP leadership convention. It was my first federal convention and it was a lot of fun. After disappointing results in the 1974 federal election, David Lewis resigned from the leadership. I quickly decided that I was supporting Ed Broadbent. As far as I can remember, most Albertans at that convention followed suit.

Ed's main competition was Rosemary Brown, a more radical B.C. NDP MLA, and Lorne Nystrom, a younger and more moderate Saskatchewan NDP MP. I felt Broadbent was more experienced as a house leader and had held on to his Oshawa, Ontario seat through that tough election.

That fall, Grant Notley and I started on my most important task as provincial secretary: fundraising. Every available night, Grant and I would hop in the car and drive out to communities around Edmonton, usually within 90 minutes of town, to do town hall-style speaking engagements.

We'd advertised our event beforehand. On average, 50-60 people would attend. Grant would go on stage and give a talk about the issues of the day. Grant didn't start off as a great speaker, but had learned the art very well by the time I showed up.

Then I would go on and give "the pitch" and ask for donations. To warm up, I retold my adventure of canvassing with Jim Staples in 1971. Then I'd make the point that our campaigns cost money, and our campaign wouldn't be funded by Imperial Oil, unlike the PC's. But if you wanted a Grant Notley to stand up for you, we'd need donations from regular Albertans.

And they did donate, often quite generously. The money we collected at these meetings kept the party alive. I think people saw the value of a strong NDP MLA to stand up to the ballooning PC caucus and a decaying Social Credit contingent.

Grant and I became very close friends during these trips together. Grant was a political animal, and these trips fed that impulse. I found it exhilarating. I was working for a cause I believed in, and how many people can say that?

We also did a lot of prospecting for candidates for both the provincial and federal NDP sections. We didn't know it at the time, but one visit in 1977 would pay off for the party some time in the future. We met with a young University of Alberta student leader named Brian Mason to talk him into running for the Federal NDP in the 1979 election. Brian wasn't a member of the party at that point, but Grant and I felt that we needed to get a new generation of candidates and activists. He turned us down.

The job came with a lot of administrative work too, and I didn't enjoy that as much. But I got along well with my staff as well as the people who worked at Grant's office in the Legislature.

After I finished that first year, I knew I wasn't going back to Calgary to return to education. Political organizing was just too exciting and addictive. The game was a serious adrenaline rush and teaching and counselling simply didn't give me that. I told the Calgary School Board that I wasn't coming back, and Edmonton very quickly came to feel like home.

At about the same time, my wife and I had to divorce. There's no point in going into the details, but I will say this: it wasn't over politics. Ede was (and is) just as solid a New Democrat as I am. It wasn't anyone's fault; it was simply the right move for both of us.

There was no issue over child custody; I knew I was on the road a lot. I could see the kids whenever I wanted to. I dealt with the emotional aftermath by throwing myself into my work and spent more time travelling with Grant.

I didn't stay single for long. I had stayed in touch with a lot of Calgary friends, and Cheryl Matheson was one of them. She also went through a divorce in 1972. She had been teaching English as a Second Language (ESL) classes, but firmly wanted to move on to something else.

Later in 1976, we started dating and she moved in with me into a new duplex home in St. Albert, a suburb north of Edmonton. She enrolled at the University of Alberta law school, and in 1977, we got married in our home, with Grant as my best man.

Cheryl was a great activist in the NDP, even before we married. She would have been a fantastic candidate, but you didn't see husband and wife political teams then like you do now (i.e. Jack Layton and Olivia Chow). She served on numerous NDP councils and committees. Through all my campaigns, she was my favourite canvassing partner.

During the 1980s, she reduced her involvement in the NDP, partially for career reasons, and partially to avoid a conflict of interest. Still, she served as a federal NDP council member and was involved in my riding campaigns.

Cheryl and I had a powerful relationship. We were drawn together through our shared values. She was my best friend.

Cheryl had three children from her previous marriage as well: Barrett, Cathy and Matt. As far as we were concerned, we were parents of all five children. They all already knew each other from the beginning of their lives. They were all friends, and still are today. Matt and Dawn would both go on to work on my leader's tour. Whenever I was running, they'd all make the trip up to volunteer in the local campaign office for at least a weekend.

While she was at law school, Cheryl and I made a close friend in Jack Harris. Jack went on to also become an NDP Leader in Newfoundland and Labrador in the late 1980s and 1990s. He was elected in 2008 as a St. John's Member of Parliament. I do regret that I didn't get to sit as an M.P. alongside him.

I had one nasty confrontation during my time as provincial secretary. A Trotskyite faction was attempting to exert influence over the Alberta NDP, and it boiled over at a provincial council meeting.

Trotskyism is an approach to communism named after Leo Trotsky. Followers of Trotsky try to pressure non-communist groups into adopting their ideals using a tactic called "entryism".

In this case, they took out NDP memberships and got control over some of our internal committees and riding associations. They would use them as bully pulpits to spout their particular brand of craziness. During the 1970s, this was causing headaches for a number of social democratic parties around the world, and we were no exception.

Most of the time, the Trotskyites attempting to inflict themselves on the Alberta NDP were easy to spot. These people often dressed, spoke and acted in a socially awkward fashion, and didn't garner the attention they craved. But there was one exception in our case.

Donald Tapscott was a good looking and sharply dressed guy. In spite of his bizarre political beliefs at the time, he was talented at getting his quotes in the media, and his communist ideology cast a very bad reflection on the party. I decided that I had to take some drastic action in his case.

The Provincial Council is a body of delegates from each riding association which meets roughly every quarter-year. It handles non-policy decisions in provincial NDP sections. I decided that I would have a motion brought to council to expel Tapscott from the NDP.

My rationale was this: The back of every NDP membership card requires the member to sign a declaration that they are not a member of another political party. This was a measure brought in decades ago across the country to keep communists out of the NDP.

By virtue of Tapscott being a member of Trotskyite organizations, he had violated that declaration. It would be a difficult confrontation, but I had no doubt that it was necessary.

As you can imagine, it was a hard debate that day. But when the vote finally came, the council overwhelming voted to expel Tapscott. Grant kidded me afterwards: "Ohhh Martin, you got blood on your hands."

I don't apologize if this seems heavy-handed. There should always be room for debate within a social democratic party. But not for those who don't respect our party's values and traditions, and communism has never had a place in the NDP's traditions any more than unfettered capitalism has. If you want a communist party, go start your own.

With his expulsion, the Trotskyites largely moved on. But Tapscott became a mogul and a celebrity. He's now a professor at the University of Toronto, a member of the World Economic Forum and owns many successful businesses. He tours the world and lectures on internet commerce. Years later, we did meet again, buried the hatchet, and had a laugh about it.

Part 5: The Legislature

March 1979 would bring the next provincial election, and we were well into organizing for it by 1978. It was going to be daunting.

Peter Lougheed was as popular as ever. Though fundraising had gone well, our available funds were a fraction of the PC's. We were nevertheless determined to gain seats in Edmonton and Northern Alberta, where Grant and I had been touring heavily.

Grant and I continued to tour. I started getting media attention in my role as provincial secretary. I would do the interviews that Grant couldn't and got some name recognition in my own right. In the fall of 1978, we decided that I should run in the north-end riding of Edmonton Norwood.

It had been a riding where the NDP had results that were better than average, and we had long decided that we would make it a priority in terms of allocating our meagre funds and resources. But we hadn't attracted a major candidate.

If you're not familiar with the neighbourhood, Norwood is a blue-collar area of Edmonton, just north of downtown. Landmarks like Commonwealth Stadium, the Northern Alberta Institute of Technology (NAIT) and the Avenue of Champions are all in Norwood.

It does have its perennial problems. Prostitution and a lack of affordable housing have plagued the area as long as I've been around. But the people there are friendly and community-minded. There are families who've been there for 40 years or more.

Cheryl and I quickly moved there from St. Albert and bought a house. We loved our home and neighbourhood, and Cheryl became very involved in neighbourhood activism in the 1980s and 1990s. To this day, I still live just a few blocks south of Norwood.

I threw myself into door-to-door canvassing. As a result, I didn't have much of a hand in the NDP's central campaign. While I was well-known in NDP circles and in the media, Norwood was a different matter. I hadn't been a part of the lives of those long-standing Norwood families yet. I was also up against a PC incumbent in Catharine Chichak, who could associate herself with her popular leader, Peter Lougheed. Door-knocking was all I did during that election campaign.

It worked, but only so well. On election night, I got 38.4% of the vote, but that was only good enough for a respectable second place. The overall results didn't bring any better news. Grant was re-elected, this time by a much healthier margin. But once again, he was the only New Democrat.

Four Social Credit MLAs were re-elected. The party of Aberhart and Manning, who had governed the province almost unopposed for 36 years, was dying rapidly. Our own campaign had pretty much ignored them.

The Progressive Conservatives won every other seat again. Grant went back into the Legislature and handled them as well as anyone could have, He used his access to the Legislature Press Gallery as best as he could. With a dying Social Credit Party, Grant was the official opposition in reality.

After that election, I decided not to return to my job as provincial secretary of the Alberta NDP. I needed a real job again.

I was hired as a guidance counsellor at Salisbury High School in Sherwood Park, a bedroom community east of Edmonton. After four years away, I found that teaching and counselling was very satisfying, although I missed being on the road with Grant. I didn't coach though. My evenings and weekends were still reserved for NDP work.

Shortly after that 1979 election, we had an NDP convention coming. Anne Hemingway was the incumbent president of the party, and I thought she was a good one. A party president doesn't wield a lot of formal authority over a political party, but they do have a lot of influence. They chair all executive, council and convention meetings.

Grant approached me to run for that position. I told him that I'd do it, but only if Anne wasn't running. Unknown to me, he also asked Alex MacEachren, a veteran candidate and activist (and future MLA).

Anne was planning to run for re-election, but I didn't know that. I also didn't know that Grant had decided that a contested presidential election would drum up some interest in that convention and boost attendance. All three of us went to the convention without realizing that the others were running.

We didn't catch him out until we were all registered as candidates. I wound up winning, but Alex was angry, and understandably so. This stunt was pretty typical for Grant, so I got over it.

My time as president was otherwise largely uneventful. I spent the majority of the next three years teaching, parenting and campaigning in Norwood, and doing my presidential duties.

There was one tense night in early 1982. There had been a fight brewing between Saskatchewan NDP Premier Allan Blakeney and Federal

NDP Leader Ed Broadbent over issues such as the Charter of Rights, the repatriation of the Constitution, and the National Energy Program. As Alberta NDP Leader, Grant was caught in the middle.

Grant decided that he would at least try to act as peacemaker. We arranged to get the provincial NDP leaders for the prairies into the same hotel meeting room as Ed Broadbent near the Calgary Airport. Despite going very late into the night, it wasn't successful. In fact, I remember then-NDP Cabinet Minister Roy Romanow almost getting in a fight with Federal NDP staffer Norm Simons. After all that, I still had to drive back to Edmonton to work at Salisbury High School the following morning.

Grant had to wind up siding with Allan Blakeney. These issues would be hashed out at a subsequent national NDP convention in 1983 in Regina, which I went to. It was a great debate with fantastic speakers like Tommy Douglas and Lorne Nystrom.

At the end of that debate, the convention delegates were fractured, as well as exhausted and irritated with each other. Douglas then gave one of his amazing keynote speeches that healed those wounds and brought the crowd to a standing ovation.

In Alberta, the media and the oil industry were especially preoccupied with the National Energy Program (NEP), and Prime Minister Pierre Trudeau's attempt to take control of distributing energy revenue, largely coming from my province.

Grant agreed that oil revenue belonged to Albertans, but he didn't share Peter Lougheed's obsession with the issue. Moreover, Grant didn't have much trust in the PCs to do anything useful with that revenue.

From my perspective, it wasn't the huge issue that some historians now claim it was. On the far right-wing of Alberta politics, there were certainly people furious with Trudeau, but the Norwood voters that I talked to weren't all that preoccupied with the NEP. As party president, I felt New Democrats agreed with Grant, but it wasn't the burning issue on their minds either.

During 1981 and 1982, there was also the right-wing phenomenon of the Western Canada Concept Party (WCC). Much like the Parti Quebecois in Quebec, they used issues like the NEP to justify the separation of the four western Canadian provinces from the rest of Canada.

They caught fire when their leader, Gordon Kessler, won a by-election in Olds-Didsbury in central rural Alberta in 1981 (Olds was Grant's hometown and it had been one of the few remaining Social Credit seats).

Kessler often struggled to keep up with the workings of the Legislature. While Kessler's views were at odds with NDP views, Grant would help him out with house procedure and rules. When there's only a handful of opposition MLAs in the Legislature, you tend to stick together despite ideological differences.

Grant and I watched a rally the WCC held in Edmonton's Jubilee Auditorium. They packed the large room and the support for their far-right rhetoric was scary. For a moment, they looked like they could do some real damage.

The rise of the WCC also spelled the end of the Social Credit Party. Two of their three remaining MLAs, Ray Speaker and Dr. Walt Buck, a Sherwood Park dentist-turned-MLA, would run as independents. Social Credit became a fringe party and remains one to this day.

After three and a half years of waiting, an election was called for November of 1982, and I would have my second chance of winning Edmonton-Norwood. I was relieved when the election was called. When you're a candidate, you tend to feel relief more than anything when an election starts because you know that there's an end in sight, win or lose.

I badly wanted to win. I had spent three years working hard on door-to-door canvassing and building recognition with the help of Cheryl and Barrett, one of Cheryl's kids. This was going to be my final attempt at becoming a MLA. If I lost again, I would just go back to education permanently.

Right off the start, I had a surprise. PC incumbent MLA Catherine Chichak decided not to run again. She would win a school board seat the following year. She was replaced with Tony Falcone.

In Norwood, the dominant issue was interest rates, as it was across the province. They had reached 20% and had a huge impact on Alberta mortgages and housing costs. Many Albertans had to walk away from their houses.

Peter Lougheed handled the interest rate issue in a masterful fashion. Mid-way through the campaign, he announced an Interest Rate Protection Program, reassuring homeowners that they would be able to afford their mortgages. At that point, his Achilles' heel was turned into his advantage. It knocked the wind out of our campaign, and I think it also put an end to the WCC.

By Election Day, I was tired and wasn't that excited about seeing the results. But at the end of the day, I met Barrett, who lifted my spirits a little while we waited for results to come in. I wound up winning by a razor-thin margin of 75 votes. Tony Falcone, the losing PC candidate, threatened to pursue a recount, but I don't think he ever did.

Any excitement I had was dashed after seeing the provincial results. Grant had barely held on to his seat, and that was it for NDP MLAs. Grant would famously quip "I don't mind giving up a few of my votes (in Spirit River-Fairview) to get Ray Martin elected." But behind his jokes, he was severely disappointed with only two seats.

The NDP had entered this election convinced that we would at least see Gordon Wright win in Edmonton-Strathcona and Alex MacEachren win in Edmonton-Kingsway. They both came close, but I think they were done in by Lougheed's mortgage announcement. In the days after, I was happy to be an MLA, but the cloud of our unfulfilled expectations hung over our heads.

We were snapped out of our depression very quickly by a new challenge. While we only had two seats, we were nonetheless the second-largest caucus in the Legislature. Therefore, we assumed that Grant would take on the title of Leader of the Opposition, and staffing, budget, and Question Period time that came with it. But we weren't the only opposition MLAs elected.

Former Social Credit MLAs Ray Speaker and Walt Buck had won their seats as independents. After Election Day, they quickly formed their own impromptu political party: The Representative Party. They made Speaker the leader and claimed that they should have the title of Leader of the Opposition by virtue of the fact that they were now tied with the NDP and that Speaker had held the position previously in the last Legislature.

The "referee" in this dispute was the Speaker of the Legislature, Gerry Amerongen. For reasons that I will never understand, he refused to make a decision until the Legislature reconvened, which meant six months of waiting and wrangling with the "Representative Party." Ross Harvey, who had moved from NDP party office staff to caucus, did a lot of work to make sure we put forward the strongest possible case.

It's been speculated that Amerongen had deliberately delayed his ruling because he and Notley did not see eye-to-eye. I don't know if this is true or not, but I certainly agree that the delay was unnecessary. When he finally ruled in our favour in March of 1983, we were ecstatic.

With that, Grant and I got to work on our first session in the Legislature. After 12 years of sitting in that chamber as a caucus of one, Grant joked that he felt like he now had "a whole horde of people with him." In reality, my presence freed him up to do a lot more of the work that comes with the title of leadership.

We had been fast friends before and being a caucus of two didn't change that. We seldom had any disagreements. Grant's biographer, Howard Leeson, would go on to write in 1992 that Grant and I had some friction over Grant's leadership issues, but we were "working it out."

I don't recall having any disputes about leadership. It was all Grant's, and the prospect of being a leader never entered my head. Maybe Grant had said something to that effect to Leeson, who was a NDP staffer at the time. I can say that Leeson's book on Grant is otherwise correct, at least for the parts that I was around for.

For his part, Grant encouraged me to get all the publicity I could. I was quite content with the way things were going; apart from the fact I wanted to see more NDP MLAs.

I did have a huge learning curve to cover though. Grant had given me 16 critic portfolios. Learning parliamentary rules is a challenge for anyone. On any day the Legislature sat, I would be making as many as 10 or 11 speeches a day, plus question period. It made for quite a grind, and I'd be thrilled when the session would end.

If you're going survive as a rookie opposition MLA in Alberta, you have to be a team player and work well with your caucus mates. You need to keep up with your work in your constituency, such as door-knocking and getting to community events. And you have to be yourself. If you do this, you'll be effective as well as have a fighting chance at being re-elected. Fortunately, I learned this early in my first term.

I may have been up against 75 PC MLAs, but I didn't feel intimidated. On my first day in Question Period, I went after Premier Lougheed. I quickly developed the reputation as a shit-disturber during my first session.

During one particularly heated debate, I lost my temper and decided to walk out, but I stormed out the wrong door. Instead of exiting through the lobby doors behind me, I stormed out through the front door. This is a big procedural violation, but the Sergeant-at-Arms didn't stop me. PC Cabinet Minister David King claimed that I had effectively resigned my seat by doing so, which was nonsense.

The stunt attracted a lot of attention. Grant had been away for that day. When he got back, he joked: "I go away for one day, and Martin goes crazy." The following week, Grant and I boycotted Question Period for an entire week to protest Amerongen's rulings in the Legislature.

We had a lot of problems with Amerongen during that term. In Canada, speakers almost always come from the government caucus, and Alberta is no exception. It's normal for opposition parties to chafe under the rulings of the speakers. But with just Grant and I on the NDP bench, we had to go to some extreme measures if we were going to shake things up in the Alberta Legislature.

I would get a lot of heckling when I spoke as well. On one occasion, I was being completely drowned out by racket coming out of the PC benches, and the Speaker couldn't settle them down. I refused to continue and told the Speaker: "I'm going to wait until the baboons settle down." Predictably, this got instant complaints from the PC House Leader, and I was told to apologize. I responded by apologizing for insulting baboons.

Grant and I were fortunate to have some great staff working with us during that term. People like Ross Harvey, Pam Barrett and Tom Sigurdson were all easy to work with, and kept Grant and I well-armed in the Legislature. They were ambitious, fun and would soon be fine elected officials in their own right.

But Grant was getting a little fatigued. One night, he and I were driving back from a meeting of the Heritage Trust Fund Committee. He told me he was thinking of making the 1986 election his last as leader. After that, he planned to run for Member of Parliament for Peace River.

Grant's leadership would end far more tragically than that.

On Friday, October 19, 1984 Grant and I had lunch in the downstairs of the Legislature. The fall session was almost done, and we talked a bit about his travel plans for the weekend. He was headed to the NDP provincial office for a meeting that was expected to go late and would fly home to Fairview the following morning.

Later in the evening, at around 11:00 PM, I got a call from Premier Lougheed's executive assistant, Bob Giffen. There had been a plane crash on the route that Grant normally took, and Giffen wanted to know if Grant had been on the flight. I told him that as far I knew, he wasn't. I went to bed without giving it a lot of thought.

At around 7:00 a.m. the next morning, I got another call from Giffen. He confirmed that Grant had been on that very flight. I didn't know this, but Grant's meeting had wrapped up earlier than he had expected, and he had made that late flight after all. Just 45 minutes after take-off, it had crashed outside of Slave Lake.

Giffen told me that some passengers had survived, and some hadn't, but he didn't know what had happened to Grant. He would call back when he knew.

The phone rang again at 10:00 a.m. "Got bad news for you …."

Part 6: Leadership

It was such a huge shock. I instantly went off my rocker with grief.

Fortunately, Cheryl was with me, and got me refocused. She said to me "Look, you've got to get it together. You're going to have to deal with the media." She was right.

I also had to break the news to the Notley family. I called their home, and Grant's 20-year-old daughter Rachel picked it up. It was a very hard phone call to make, yet I had no choice but to deliver the news.

The week that followed was brutally difficult, but it also amazed me. The reaction from the public was astounding, and it would have astounded Grant as well. The province went into profound collective shock and mourning like I hadn't seen before.

For those too young to have been there, it was something like the passing of Jack Layton in 2011. I can only guess at the reasons why. Even though the NDP under Grant's leadership had never gotten more than 16% support, Albertans took a lot of comfort that he was there for them, standing up against the PC juggernaut, unafraid. They respected him and knew he was someone special. And I think that will be his legacy for a long time to come.

A funeral was held in Edmonton and the burial was held in Fairview, where he lived. Of all places, it was there that I got to see the humanity of Peter Lougheed. He had allowed the government plane to be used to fly in NDP leaders from across the county so that they could be there as well. He stood next to me during that day, with tears in his eyes.

When the Legislature reconvened, there was a memorial for Grant. As I stood next to Grant's empty desk, the Sergeant-at-Arms Oscar Lacombe, a very formal ex-military man, saluted his seat. I very nearly lost it again at that moment.

It's wonderful that his life is celebrated by young Alberta New Democrats who weren't even born when Grant was around. I think it's vital that our party knows its history and its personalities like Tommy Douglas, David Lewis and Grant.

There are trials in any political life, but that was a tough one. There's no trick to getting through a tragedy likes Grant's death, you just keep busy and try not to dwell on the grief.

There had already been a NDP convention planned for the weekend of November 9th. It would now serve as a leadership convention. It was fairly obvious that leadership was going to land on my shoulders, but that doesn't mean that there weren't plenty of New Democrats with misgivings about me. There had been an entire generation of NDP members who had never known any other leader but Grant, and I had barely two years of experience as an MLA.

Out of the party executive, there were some who were nervous at the prospect of making me leader so quickly. It was Party President Don Aitken and Grant's widow Sandy Notley who both stood up for me, and that helped considerably.

Leadership is a big responsibility, and I didn't have time for self-doubt. The Legislative session would reconvene, but it was also already close to finished, and there was little appetite from any MLA to extend any longer than necessary.

The first job that winter was obvious. There would be a by-election in Spirit River-Fairview. For the NDP, losing that seat simply could not happen.

Sandy Notley and NDP organizers like Provincial Secretary Bill Dryden had firmly made up their minds who they wanted replacing Grant as MLA. Betty MacArthur had been a close friend and ally to the Notleys, and she had gotten a very public blessing from Sandy.

I tried to stay out of it, but I certainly knew how Sandy felt. And I knew at the time that Betty had challengers for that NDP nomination, but I didn't know them. I travelled to Fairview to attend that nomination meeting and thought Betty's nomination would be a done deal. And I was wrong.

Local teacher Jim Gurnett won that nomination. It came as a huge shock to the Notleys and the staff. I didn't know Jim at all, but his speech at that meeting had impressed me.

That surprise turned out to be a good one. Jim impressed me with his integrity, excellent speaking ability, and honesty. He turned out to be a natural, and Sandy was quickly won over as well.

The by-election happened quickly afterwards. We threw every resource we had into it. I spent a lot of time in the Peace River region, door knocking before and during the by-election period. On February 21, Jim narrowly pulled it off, and I was relieved and happy. During that by-election, I also had the birth of my first grandchild, Justin, to celebrate.

When Jim arrived at the Legislature, he turned out to be a quick study and a great MLA. He delivered solid speeches and became confident on his feet very quickly. Jim's style wasn't as aggressive as mine. He was (and is) more of a statesman than I am.

I was then freed up to concentrate on leadership duties. Surprisingly, I found that I enjoyed leadership, almost every minute of it. I was especially stimulated by doing the public speaking and the media hits.

The spring and summer of 1985 were predictably busy. The Legislature reconvened very shortly after the by-election, and Jim and I were always tied up by our daily loads of 10 speeches and 10 questions every day, and the preparation that came with it.

We were successful in getting a lot of media attention. But I was relieved when it wrapped up at the end of the spring.

And it was at that time Lougheed announced that he was stepping down from his premiership. I think he knew the economic downturn that was on its way and decided that he didn't need to stick around for it.

In 2012, a political magazine called "Policy Options" put Lougheed on the cover and declared him the best premier in Canada's last 50 years. Personally, I think that these comparisons are impossible, especially when you consider how different Canada's provinces are from each other. How can you compare the effectiveness of Lougheed, who governed a province with lots of revenue, to a Saskatchewan premier like Romanow, who took over a bankrupted province and brought it back to fiscal and economic health?

There's no doubt that Peter Lougheed left office in 1985 looking very good. But it's not hard to look good when you govern a resource-rich province like Alberta. That being said, I'll concede that he was a very politically able premier. I've got a lot of respect for him, especially for his help when we were mourning Grant's passing.

Conversely, I knew that the subsequent PC leadership race was probably going to drown out anything Jim and I would do for media attention during that summer. It was time to hit the road.

Knowing an election would definitely come in 1986, I decided to spend the summer of 1985 touring every inch of Alberta that I could get to. The party rented a mobile home and drove from town to town. I met with almost anyone we could get our hands on.

I got trotted out in front of municipal government officials, party activists, town hall meetings, and anywhere else that had a crowd. I had one staffer, John Heaney, to help me out. I probably could have flown to some of these trips, but I like the road better. This is where I got my leadership training that would carry me through the years to come.

The Alberta Progressive Conservatives were facing life without Lougheed for the first time in a generation. Three candidates stepped up: Don Getty, a former star Edmonton Eskimos quarterback and former cabinet minister; Ron Ghitter, the only Calgary candidate; and my old frat brother, Julian Koziak, who now was the Minister of Education.

Ghitter was branded as "Calgary's candidate" and probably the candidate I least wanted to face. He was a great communicator and would have been difficult to tangle with in the Legislature and in the next campaign. Julian Koziak never wrestled the Edmonton vote away from Getty and I didn't see him as likely to win the leadership.

When the PC leadership vote came in October of 1985, Don Getty won. He was quickly sworn in as premier and my opponent in the next election, which I thought was good news. Words simply didn't flow smoothly out of Getty like they did from Lougheed or Ghitter.

Sometimes, he made statements that didn't make sense. I found that you could rattle him by being a little aggressive in Question Period and other forums. He would try to respond with the same aggression and that's where he'd say something he'd regret.

While the tiny NDP caucus was going through all this upheaval, the Representative caucus was soldiering on into the election as well, trying to form an alternative to the PCs. Ray Speaker, a more hard-line conservative, continued as leader.

They remained our allies in a sense. Walt Buck, a veteran of the Legislature dating back to 1967, was even a friend to me. He would sell my first golf club membership. We kept in touch for decades afterwards. They were trying to turn the Representative Party into a properly organized party, but I don't think they really put a lot into that effort. Still, they were very popular in their own constituencies, and perhaps deservedly so.

The Liberals were a different matter. They hadn't held a seat in the Legislature since 1971. Nick Taylor had taken over leadership and soldiered on, overshadowed by Pierre Trudeau and the Liberal brand's unpopularity in Alberta during the 1970s and 1980s.

It's easy to like Nick Taylor. He had a great sense of humour. He also recruited quality candidates with a good work ethic, like Grant Mitchell, who was challenging the PC Speaker, Gerry Amerongen, in

Edmonton Meadowlark. He carried out an intense door-to-door canvassing campaign, much like the ones that the NDP would launch years later to get David Eggen and Deron Bilous elected.

Before an election started, the great NDP icon, Tommy Douglas, passed away. I went to the funeral. It was a huge event, as you'd expect. Tommy had been a great supporter of the Alberta section of the NDP, especially of Grant. He would go to all of Grant's nomination meetings, and he and I would usually chat there.

For those generations of New Democrats who've never known Tommy Douglas as anything other than a legend, I can only describe him as just a really nice man. He never put on airs. He was an amazing speaker; you could feel electricity in a room after he spoke.

New Democrats got a sneak preview of the political change to come in Edmonton in a federal by-election held in April. Long-time PC M.P. Peter Elzinga resigned his west Edmonton area seat of Pembina. Ivor Dent, the former mayor of Edmonton, came out of political retirement to run for the NDP, in spite of the riding having voted 70% PC in the last election. I think he sensed the NDP's impending growth in Edmonton and decided to take advantage of it.

Dent was a great New Democrat and a great guy to be around. He had been an alderman and was mayor of Edmonton from 1968 to 1974, before I moved there. He had led Edmonton to winning the 1977 Commonwealth Games and the building of Commonwealth Stadium. Grant and I would visit with him often.

I pitched in on campaigning for Ivor. He came very close to winning, just 300 odd votes behind the PC's Walt van de Walle. It's a shame and I think he would've been great as a Member of Parliament.

I was excited when the provincial election finally kicked off in April, but just at the prospect of winning only seven seats. Throughout the pre-election campaign, seven seats were all we thought possible to hold, and was what we focused our time and resources on.

Four of them had been in Edmonton, including my seat. We also expected Jim Gurnett to be re-elected in Spirit River-Fairview and new seats in Vegreville-Viking with Derek Fox and Bob Hawkesworth in Calgary, who gave us real creditability in that city. Quite frankly, I'd have even been happy with four of us sneaking into the Legislature.

We made one major change to our platform and communications campaign compared to Grant's previous campaign: we wanted to stay positive at every chance. Our campaign tagline was "Send them a message", which is a common NDP theme. But unlike previous campaigns, we always tried to accompany it with a positive policy alternative, rather than just list off PC sins.

1986 proved to be a fun and easy campaign for me. I found that being the leader was easier than my three previous campaigns as a local riding candidate. Touring on the bus and doing media hits were a lot more stimulating than canvassing day after day. It was easy to get enthused about doing media events, and it helped that I'm a good napper, and sleep easily in cars and buses.

My local campaign in Edmonton-Norwood, managed by my constituency assistant George Oleksiuk, was working hard towards re-election. Remember, I had only won in 1982 by 75 votes. I shouldn't have worried. Norwood door-knocking was the easiest I'd ever seen it, before or since. Every talk with a voter seemed to end in a NDP vote. It was a love-in.

The media had been positive and receptive, and the supporters I had met at events across the province were bursting with enthusiasm. Albertans were saddled with high unemployment, terrible grain prices, and were watching a lackluster PC campaign. They were in a mood to listen to the NDP, more so than any other point in history. We had a simple message to counter Don Getty's bad communication.

We ended the campaign with an amazing event just before Election Day. By 1986, k.d. lang was a huge country music star, both in Alberta and just about everywhere else. She agreed to do an impromptu free concert on a street in downtown Edmonton for our campaign at our last rally. A huge crowd of young people stretched out in all directions. It was exhilarating for me and I've no doubt it helped end the campaign with momentum.

This was in contrast to a similar event that the PCs had put on for Getty. Instead of going with a hip, rising star like Lang, they brought out Bobby Curtola, a fairly tame pop star from the early 1960s.

In the end, it's true what they say: The big moments like this just wind up being a blur. I learned that on election night, in 1986.

We were in a room in the Sands Hotel. It's just south of the Yellowhead Trail in north Edmonton to this day. Cheryl was there. To tell you the truth, she had probably anticipated this breakthrough more than me.

The results started coming in, and so did the surprises. And that's when the memories become fuzzy.

I had been in my riding all of Election Day, and I was no longer concerned for my own seat of Edmonton-Norwood. Sure enough, I won with 61% of the vote. All but one of our priority ridings were won quickly and easily. It was then that the surprise wins all over Edmonton started pouring in.

Of the record sixteen seats we won that night, the biggest surprise was Marie Laing. She was our candidate in the southern suburban riding of Edmonton-Avonmore. She had been pursuing her Ph.D. at the time. To convince her to run, I had specifically promised her that she would *not* win.

In fact, she had spent Election Day volunteering for Gordon Wright, her neighbouring Edmonton-Strathcona candidate. She got the "happy news" from a reporter who famously asked her in a parking lot how it felt to be a newly-elected MLA. Stunned, Marie responded with dead silence.

Once watching the results were finished, I went down to meet an ecstatic ballroom filled with 600 NDP supporters. On that stage, I said "How sweet it is!" and the crowd went nuts. I don't remember much else I said from the stage.

Apparently, I talked about Grant, who was very much in my thoughts that evening. I also talked about Jim Gurnett, who somehow lost his seat that night. It hurt, because I thought he had deserved to win. He had been a fantastic partner in the legislature after he had taken over from Grant as Spirit River-Fairview MLA. Even though Grant had struggled sometimes to win the riding, I thought Jim was as popular in those communities.

I announced that the next election would result in an NDP government. And that night I think everyone in that room probably agreed with me.

After coming down from that stage, I remember even less. It just seemed that people were all over me with joy in their voices. I know I did a press scrum, but I don't remember the questions or answers. I know I talked to all sorts of members, volunteers, donors and activists; but I can't remember the conversations.

I remember feeling like the world was our oyster. I remember feeling that government was inevitably next. I just remember feeling that anything *was* possible.

That's the feeling that I recall from that night, the absolute excitement and joy that was in that room. That's what stays with me. It's a feeling that maybe happens to you once in a lifetime.

It didn't fade quickly. The next day was filled with media interviews, and I tasked a very excited Ross Harvey with transitioning 15 new MLAs into the Legislature. The new caucus met less than a week after the election.

For some, like Gordon Wright and Alex McEachern, it was a triumphant entry after over 15 years of trying. For others, like Laing or Barry Pashak, they were still shocked to find themselves as MLAs. Unfortunately, we had little time to get them orientated, as the Legislature reconvened in June and sat throughout the summer. We put Jim Gurnett on a contract to do training and orientation with the new MLAs. I quickly felt pretty confident in this group.

During that time, there were a few immediate changes in my life. First of all, I had a lot more media to do on a day-to-day basis. I also was able to shed myself of the dozen or so shadow cabinet portfolios that I had necessarily carried for the past four years. I then got to hand out those jobs to the new caucus.

Pam Barrett made for a sharp House Leader. She had beaten a cabinet minister in Edmonton-Highlands after serving as a staffer in the Alberta Federation of Labour and for the NDP caucus at the Legislature. She was very articulate, quick on her feet, and was good at negotiating with the other parties. We didn't have a Deputy Leader in that caucus, but she served in that role for all intents and purposes.

Derek Fox was one of our two rural MLAs, elected in the Eastern Alberta riding of Vegreville-Viking. He was a beekeeper from Hairy Hill. I appointed him as Caucus Whip (or, more accurately, my problem-solver) and also gave him the tough job of Agriculture Critic, a role that's always heavy with meetings. Derek is a great person and was a natural as an elected official.

Bob Hawkesworth came in with previous experience as an elected official, having served two terms as a Calgary alderman. I suspect he ran in Calgary Mountain View in the 1986 election simply because he got tired of being harassed by me to do so. I appointed Bob to chair the caucus meetings, which was a considerably more complicated job with sixteen MLAs as opposed to two. Bob kept meetings short and focused, which was great as I don't have much tolerance for long meetings.

There were a lot of changes in other corners of the Legislature as well. In the Speaker's Chair, Gerry Amerongen had lost his seat in the Legislature and was replaced by David Carter from Calgary.

David had been a good friend of Grant's. They had travelled to Russia together. I also got along with him in his new role and he allowed me a lot of freedom in the Legislature and let me say what I wanted. But my fellow NDP MLAs felt differently, and thought he showed bias to the PC government MLAs. It's a common complaint for most opposition MLAs.

For the first time since the 1960s, there was also a Liberal caucus. After twelve years of trying, Nick Taylor finally reached the Legislature and brought three other MLAs with him, enough for party status. And Ray Speaker and Walt Buck returned to the Legislature for one final term under the Representative Party banner.

One other change came on the other side of the aisle. The PC caucus started pushing back and challenging what I had to say in the Legislature, as opposed to largely ignoring or blithely heckling me. They assigned a newly-elected Red Deer MLA by the name of Stockwell Day to be the "Ray Martin attack dog". Day's standard theme was that anything I proposed was "crazy" or "too radical".

Shortly after that election, I went to Nova Scotia to speak at their provincial NDP convention. Alexa McDonough was the leader of the party. I'd met her a few years previously along with Grant when she had visited our convention. We had commiserated together at the time about being in small one- or two-MLA caucuses. I though then (and still do) that Alexa made for a great leader.

I told the New Democrats there that if a NDP breakthrough could be won in Alberta, it could be won in Nova Scotia. They would prove me right in 1998 by winning 19 seats. In 2009, they won government.

When the Alberta Legislature reconvened, Edmonton was deep into a serious labour crisis. One of Canada's toughest strikes was already on at the Gainers' meat packing plants, owned by Peter Pocklington.

It was a scary and ugly situation on the picket line. Pocklington had decided to force scab workers through the United Food and Commercial Workers' picket line. To the union's credit, they would not back down.

I wanted to make sure the province knew whose side the NDP was on. I made sure that every NDP MLA visited that picket line to show support for the UFCW. But it was very tense. I've visited dozens of picket lines and I've never seen one that tense before or since. I thought someone was going to get hurt or killed.

Why did Gainers happen? It's because Alberta had some of the weakest labour legislation in Canada. Allowing scab labour just takes a bad situation and makes it dangerous. As people fight for their livelihood, it brings about a violent daily confrontation. Governments that allow scab labour, allow violence.

That's why the NDP chose to side with the union then and now. It's not a matter of political advantage, it's the right thing to do for the families that count on jobs that pay the bills. The Pocklingtons of the world have enough friends in Alberta's Legislature. And as Premier Getty was a good ideological friend of Pocklington's, he would effectively bribe Pocklington with millions of dollars in loans to end the strike. As of this writing, Pocklington still owes Alberta taxpayers millions of dollars.

It'll be remembered as one of Alberta's uglier moments. But I noticed that the strike created a lot of new union activists, especially amongst new Canadians. And whenever you have Albertans willing to stick up for themselves and their community, it's good news.

Cheryl also graduated with her law degree in 1986. She set up a family law practice on Alberta Avenue, right in the heart of Norwood. She would joke that she got asked to do a lot of free work for people in the neighbourhood by virtue of her husband being the local MLA. Cheryl's office became a fixture on the Avenue, and she would serve as community league president.

In early 1987, one of our rookie MLAs would land in the spotlight for a simple act that, in this day and age, no one would think twice about: he spoke in French in the Legislature.

Leo Piquette was another one of the surprise wins of the 1986 election. He won the northern riding of Athabasca-Lac la Biche. He was a Franco-Albertan farmer outside of Plamondon that Grant and I had talked into running before Grant's death. He had organized and campaigned for a couple of years prior to the election, but I still thought a victory in that riding was a bridge too far.

But Leo was in the Legislature now, and on April 7, 1987, he did something that is routine for an opposition MLA: he got up and asked a question. Only he decided to ask it in French. Leo was going to ask education minister Nancy Betkowski about education in French for Franco-Albertans. Leo knew that Betkowski understood and spoke French as well. It only made sense that he should ask his question in French.

I wasn't in the Legislature at that moment. I was in our nearby caucus office, and I hadn't given his question any more thought than any of our other MLAs' questions. I hardly speak any French myself, and I've lost what French I learned in school. It's been suggested that this day was "planned", and I can assure you it wasn't.

But when Leo stood up to ask his question, Speaker Carter cut him off twice. "En anglais, s'iv vous plait." He refused to allow Leo to ask his question in French. This would touch off a storm of controversy that would last for months, pitting French Canadians versus the more reactionary characters amongst Canadian conservatives.

I certainly don't believe that Leo caused this controversy. It was Carter's overreaction that started this upheaval. I also don't believe that Carter was or is intolerant of francophones, I think he just chose to be stubborn at a time that called for flexibility.

There was no question in caucus that all NDP MLAs and I would show their support for Leo. No one in the NDP balked at taking up his cause.

But the reactionary conservatives would make their presence known and we got some pretty ugly calls, letters, and even a few threats. But these aren't people who'd ever be likely to support us in the first place.

As for Leo himself, it took a while for him to get used to being the champion of the Alberta Francophone community, but he did it well. A couple of rallies were organized by francophone organizations and held at the Legislature to show their support for him. The issue came to a head in 1988 when a Supreme Court decision effectively allowed Legislature to make up whatever language rules they wanted.

1987 also brought one of Edmonton's worst natural disasters, a tornado that ripped through the north and east end of the city. July 31, 1987 is still called "Black Friday" by Edmontonians. I was out of the tornado's path that day, but it cut a swath of destruction along Mill Woods, Refinery Row, and worst of all in Evergreen Trailer Park.

A few days afterwards, I toured Evergreen. I was shocked at the destruction I saw, and it's a sight that stays with me to this day.

In 1987, there was another political movement kicking off in Alberta: the birth of the Reform Party. Ernest Manning's son Preston had organized a new federal political party. To tell you the truth, I paid scant attention to it. I dismissed it as a reincarnation of Gordon Kessler and the Western Canada Concept, and figured it would fizzle just as quickly.

They don't hand out too many perks to NDP leaders in Alberta, but I did get one in early 1988. Calgary hosted the world in the Winter Olympics, and I got to be around for a few events.

The Calgary Olympics weren't as controversial compared to the debates around hosting the 2010 games in Vancouver or Toronto's Olympic bids. Grant had been the lone NDP MLA when Calgary had pursued their bid in 1981 and he had supported the venture.

I didn't get to see the marquee events, like hockey games or the ceremonies. I did get to see Elizabeth Manley win her silver medal in figure skating.

While things went swimmingly in my NDP caucus, the same could not be said for Nick Taylor and the new Liberal caucus. Nick may have been a nice guy and he may have brought Liberal MLAs back to the Legislature for the first time in decades, but apparently that wasn't enough for his party members.

In 1987, Liberals voted for a leadership review. In 1988, things went from bad to worse for Nick when he had to face off with rookie MLA Grant Mitchell (who was a very hard-working MLA, much like a David Eggen or Deron Bilous is now).

It subsequently got really tough for Nick (and eventually, me) when Laurence Decore announced that he was ready to leave the Edmonton Mayor's chair to take over the Liberal party.

Decore was regarded as a capable mayor and took his share of the spotlight from Getty and myself immediately. He wasn't much of a public speaker but took a lot of attention away from us by virtue of his former office, primarily in my Edmonton "backyard" of 12 NDP seats.

I had a few people biting at my heels as well. In 1988, the media published a story about a group of "anonymous members" led by former St. Paul NDP candidate Jeff Dubois that was unhappy about my leadership and claimed that I should be replaced by union leader Reg Basken.

This "group" never appeared at a council or convention to challenge me. The media claimed that "nothing angers him (me) more" than this kind of backbiting and they're probably right. The fact that they never challenged me to my face (as they had numerous opportunities to do) was cowardly, as I see it. But Reg never seemed to have political ambitions, and it was an irritation, nothing more.

A few years later, I did face a challenge to my leadership at a convention from another St. Paul member, Don Ronaghan, but I got re-elected as leader easily, and it proved just to be another irritation.

That fall, the 1988 "Free Trade" election was called by Mulroney, and we were excited at the chance to build on our provincial success. Ross Harvey, who had been working with me as a staffer from my days as NDP provincial secretary, was ready to set off as a candidate. He ran in Edmonton East, a federal riding that overlapped with much of my own provincial seat. The Legislature didn't sit that fall, so I could pitch in on his campaign.

Ross won his seat narrowly, and we came close in a number of other ridings. I was happy for him, but I missed the great work he did for us in caucus. Ross was both a great writer and public speaker, although he would use some incredibly ornate words that would have me reaching for the dictionary from time to time.

We then had to dive into our own re-election. Getty recalled the Legislature in February of 1989, had the Lieutenant Governor deliver a throne speech, and then immediately called an election less than three years after the last one.

There are a couple of theories why Don Getty called an election so early into the term with a large majority. One is that he wanted to dodge the worst of the big Principal Group scandal. Many Albertans had invested and lost their savings with this firm, and the report on this was upcoming. I was trying to hold the Premier to account on this in Question Period, but cabinet minister Connie Osterman was the one who resigned and shouldered the blame.

Another theory is that Getty wanted to face Decore before the Liberals were properly organized around him. It was a campaign widely billed as "the race for second place" between Decore and I. His presence made the major difference for me from 1986. Getty and the PCs had a commanding lead despite his mediocre communications and his government's scandals.

Oddly enough, I don't remember the 1989 campaign as clearly as 1986 or 1993 or most other elections I worked on. I couldn't even tell you what our core message was, which should tell you something of how different this campaign was compared to my first.

I just told Albertans what a good opposition we had been and focused on touring and developing the platform. I also had the treat of having my son Matt working for the campaign and riding the tour bus with me, which made the campaign a lot more fun.

This is stating the obvious but organizing an election campaign when you lead a 16- person caucus is much easier than when it's just you and one other MLA. Nonetheless, the 1989 campaign quickly turned into a fight to keep our 16 seats, especially with Laurence Decore and the Liberals competing for the same turf.

The MLAs were upbeat about their chances for re-election. Even the "surprise MLAs" like Marie Laing had worked to build healthy riding associations and had campaigns ready to roll. But we didn't think any of them were immune from being upset by the Liberals, other than myself in Edmonton Norwood.

There were exceptions to our optimism. John Younie, our MLA for Edmonton-Glengarry and environment critic, was in the Liberal crosshairs. Laurence Decore had won the Liberal leadership, but he didn't have a seat in the Legislature. He decided to run against John. We knew that a former mayor and party leader would make for a very tough re-election for John. Undaunted, he campaigned hard anyway, to his credit.

Our "surprise" seat in St. Albert was also in jeopardy. This Edmonton bedroom community had been won by Bryan Strong, a very devoted labour leader, but he proved to be an odd fit for the Legislature.

Bryan considered himself more of a labour leader than an MLA. He certainly wasn't negligent in his duties, especially when I made him Labour critic. But he didn't have much of an interest in other issues. When his term ended, he went back to work for the labour movement instead of running for re-election.

We had some hope of gaining a few seats in Calgary, but much of our focus and concern was on keeping the incumbents we had. At various times, I felt anxious about all of our caucus being vulnerable.

All in all, for the first time in my political life, I had something to lose. It didn't cause me to panic, but it made things a little more uncomfortable for me.

Laurence Decore and I may have been competing for the same geographic pieces of Alberta turf. But when it came to values, Decore was more right wing that Don Getty. He started crafting the same themes of slashing services to Alberta families that would colour the 1993 campaign.

I didn't get to really debate Decore or Getty. We had one TV event where each of us were asked questions, but it was pretty tame. I don't think many Albertans cared.

After a quiet campaign, election night arrived. It would prove to be a night coloured by relief, as opposed to the euphoria of 1986.

Sure enough, St. Albert and Edmonton Glengarry were lost. John Younie put up a formidable fight, but Decore still won fairly easily. Unpleasant surprises came in losing Leo Piquette and Lac La Biche. Maybe "L'affaire Piquette" had a role in it. Maybe he was a fluke from the beginning. I still don't understand why he lost. Jim Gurnett had also fought like hell in 1989 to get back into the Legislature in Dunvegan-Central Peace, but for naught.

But we gained good people too. Jerry Doyle, the mayor of Edson, won the west Alberta riding of West Yellowhead. It had been a narrow loss in 1986. A big surprise was an ex-Tory school principal that I barely knew by the name of Stan Woloshyn. He won in the bedroom community of Stony Plain.

John McInnis was a special addition to the caucus for me. He narrowly won the east end riding of Edmonton Jasper Place. John was a long time NDP staffer with great ambition. He took over from John Younie as environment critic and made life miserable for the new Environment Minister, Ralph Klein.

We won sixteen seats again, and only lost 3% of our share of the vote province-wide. I barely noticed that we had slipped from 2nd place to 3rd in the popular vote. I was just thrilled to have come out ahead of Decore and the Liberals, who only rose to eight seats. We lost a lot of close races in Calgary, but Bob Hawkesworth and Barry Pashak held on.

Not many Albertans were paying attention to me that night. Most were focused on the race in Edmonton-Whitemud, a riding in the suburban southwest of Edmonton. Premier Don Getty was losing his seat to Liberal Percy Wickman. Wickman was a city councilor who knocked off a premier despite being confined to a wheelchair. It surprised me as much as anyone. I guess he had deeper roots than Getty in those neighbourhoods from his time in municipal government.

I walked out of the victory party feeling satisfied. I told CBC television that we'd done well by virtue of "holding our vote" and keeping 16 seats. I don't think I was being naïve. I knew that the Liberals were coming for our Edmonton and Calgary seats. But I thought we'd repelled them for that election, and that we'd be ok.

Maybe in the NDP we're too easily satisfied.

Once again, I got the new-ish caucus together quickly, including the three rookies. John McInnis had been bred for MLA-hood, so he jumped in with no hesitation. Jerry Doyle was a great constituency MLA, and always had a positive and loyal attitude. Stan Woloshyn seemed very cooperative and got along well with the rest of the caucus.

Not long after the 1989 provincial election was over, Alberta held municipal elections. My home riding of Edmonton Norwood was part of a hotly contested municipal race.

There were a couple of candidates with NDP membership running, including Pam Barrett's favourite, Cindy Olsen. But I decided to spend my efforts supporting a young brash bus driver named Brian Mason.

Even if Brian didn't have an NDP card in his pocket, I thought he was far better organized than the others. What impressed me the most is that he did a ton of the most important campaign activity for any candidate: door-to-door canvassing. I did some with him, and quickly saw how effective he could be at the door.

Sure enough, he won his seat on council. Brian was a great progressive voice on council, even if It meant he took heat from the media or other councilors.

That being said, most Edmonton New Democrats were more fixated on the election of Jan Reimer, our first NDP mayor since Ivor Dent. I certainly supported Jan, and I definitely think she was better than the other candidates she ran against.

Nevertheless, I didn't get along with her that well. I felt like she took the attitude that our NDP Caucus was there to take her orders and do her bidding at the Legislature. I certainly wanted to cooperate with her, but I wasn't about to take orders from City Hall. But we shared the same values, and Edmonton's a better place for having had her as mayor.

And at the end of the year, Alberta New Democrats had a choice to make: pick a leader to replace Ed Broadbent. Ed had resigned from politics after a 1988 federal campaign that had gone very well in western Canada, but not nearly well enough in Ontario or Quebec to satisfy him.

There was a big field of candidates to replace him, seven in all. I decided early on that the smart thing for me to do was to stay out of it and let the members and delegates decide for themselves. Some of our MLAs took sides, and that was fine for them, but a leader can't close doors to any member, regardless of who they pick in these contests.

That didn't mean there wasn't a candidate that I wanted to vote for. I was enthusiastic about Dave Barrett, the ex-BC NDP Premier who had shown up to so many of my nomination meetings. I was pretty bad at keeping it a secret. I may not have said it to the press gallery, but I'm sure my support for Dave was heavily gossiped.

In that day, provincial party leaders automatically got delegate status and a vote at NDP conventions, and I was there to get my vote in for Dave. It was a pretty wild convention, and it took four ballots to elect Audrey McLaughlin over Barrett.

Audrey was the MP for the Yukon. I had gotten to know her a bit before she was leader. I hadn't supported her largely out of loyalty to Dave, but also because I thought Dave understood Alberta. I thought she was a good M.P., but I had my doubts about how well she was going to do in my province.

The summer of 1990 brought a blow to the caucus. Gordon Wright was the NDP MLA for Edmonton Strathcona. While he worked as a crown prosecutor, he had been a CCF/NDP activist since the 1950s, and he had even run for the Alberta NDP leadership against Grant in 1968.

Famously, Gordon ran for office five times in Strathcona before winning a seat as an MLA in 1986. The twenty years of work and campaigning he did in that riding is a big reason why it's still the strongest NDP seat in Alberta today.

He spoke with an English accent and was the biggest physical fitness freak I ever met, well before it was fashionable. That's saying something coming from a former gym teacher.

It came as a shock when he called me up in January and told me he had pancreatic cancer. I still vividly remember what he said: "Guess what, Ray. Physical fitness isn't everything." His health declined very rapidly after that talk.

One thing about New Democrats across Canada is that we're a tight-knit bunch. We always cheer each other on, from province to province. That September, Ontario gave us a reason to cheer.

Bob Rae had been the leader of the Ontario NDP since 1982. While he wasn't a member of our little klatch of western Canadian NDP leaders, I still met up with him often at conventions and other events. We had a chat prior to his 1990 election campaign.

He had already led the NDP through two elections and was only going to lead one more campaign. He was pretty much set on returning to federal politics.

When he won a stunning majority government shortly after Labour Day, I called him up and said "Guess what Bob, you're not running federally after all." I thought I was being funny. It turns out I'm not much of a prophet.

In October of 1990, Gordon Wright died. It was a very tough time for the Alberta NDP. He had been a part of our Alberta NDP family for much longer than I. Derek Fox had been especially close with him and spoke at his funeral.

This meant we had to have yet another "must-win" by-election in Edmonton-Strathcona. The premier chooses when by-elections are called, and Don Getty didn't feel like giving us much time. The by-election was called for that December, and I was worried.

Strathcona was changing into a more progressive neighbourhood, so it was one of the few places in Alberta where the PCs didn't have much of a chance. But Decore and the Liberals certainly did. They remained a serious challenge to us in Edmonton. I was worried they'd swoop in and run away with the seat. If we were going to remain credible as the official opposition, we had to win.

We recruited Barrie Chivers to run for us. Barrie was a good friend of Gord Wright's and a prominent labour lawyer with his practice in the riding. I spent a lot of time door-knocking with Barrie that winter. It paid off. Barrie won with over 50% of the vote, and I got a first-rate new MLA.

In October of 1991, within four days of each other, both of Alberta's neighbouring provinces got NDP governments. Mike Harcourt was elected in B.C. and Roy Romanow in Saskatchewan. Once again, I was making congratulatory calls to two great guys and fine premiers.

It was at this time that I felt there was a chance, albeit a narrow one, that we could form a government in Alberta. It seems crazy now, but at that point we were surrounded by NDP governments, we had our first NDP Member of Parliament with Ross Harvey, and I was being handed polls that said we were in an effective three-way tie with the PCs and the Liberals.

I decided to be prepared. I called on an old friend who had a little bit of experience with being in an Alberta government, former PC MLA Cal Lee. I had him draw up a very brief transition plan, just to be safe.

What would an Alberta NDP government in 1993 look like? It's not something I think about too much, but I've been asked that question.

I think you would have had a government that would have eliminated the deficit much more quickly without making Albertan's working families and poor pay so much of the burden. We would have done this by retaining more of the royalties from Alberta's resource extraction and keeping a progressive income tax instead of a flat income tax. I think this would have led to the sort of economic renewal that we saw in Saskatchewan under Romanow and Calvert.

Also, like Romanow, we would have made the expansion of access to health clinic a priority. Alberta has many rural communities that aren't big enough to support a hospital but needed a public health clinic.

Those would have been the priorities. But we'll never know if it would've had the positive impact I think it would.

1992 is when we started planning for another election. And it's also when things started to fall apart.

Since 1986, the caucus had got along well and worked together as a team. That came to a halt when Gerry Gibeault decided to take aim at the housing allowances that MLAs from outside Edmonton get to have apartments near the Legislature.

Gerry was the NDP MLA for Edmonton Mill Woods, a large southeast Edmonton suburb. He had been another surprise in the sweep of 1986, and he liked to think of himself as the conscience of the caucus. He was, as a result, a bit of a lone wolf.

And maybe that's what drove Gerry's public tirade. He was upset that MLAs that represented Edmonton's bedroom communities like Sherwood Park or Leduc still got the housing allowance, even though their commute wasn't very long. He went so far as to call them "pigs at the trough."

The problem was that one of those MLAs was also a New Democrat. Stan Woloshyn represented the town of Stony Plain, which is about 40 kilometers from the Legislature. It wasn't much of a surprise that Stan didn't appreciate being called a "pig". It created a lot of tension in caucus.

The next development was less of a surprise. There had been a lot of rumours for some time that Don Getty was going to step down. Things were getting tough for both him and the province. The economy was still in a bust and the blame was being laid at his feet. Decore's calls for severe cuts were gaining traction.

I think, in some ways, Don Getty never stopped being a quarterback. And quarterbacks don't like the thought of being a second-stringer. That's how Don would have felt if he had lost out on a leadership challenge or lost the next election. That's why I think he walked away when he did.

The PCs had moved away from leadership contests voted on by convention delegates to a system where every PC member got a vote. The way the PCs constructed the "run-off" system has come to make for very unpredictable results. There's a first round of voting. Unless a candidate gets over 50% of the vote (which is rare), there's a second and final round of voting with the top three "finalists". Whoever wins that, regardless if they get 50% or not, wins the PC leadership.

There were nine candidates, but I thought there were really only three cabinet ministers who had a shot at winning: Rick Orman, Nancy

Betkowski, and Ralph Klein. All three of them were effective candidates from a PC member's view, but I guessed that Betkowski was set to win, not that I had any secret information.

I was sort of right. She won the first round by one single vote, but Klein swept the second round easily. I think if all a PC member at the time cared about was winning elections, then Klein was their best choice, given his credentials as a popular Olympic mayor of Calgary and cabinet minister, and his communication skills. I don't think Betkowski would have beaten Decore in 1993.

Ralph had been a federal Liberal previously. He'd even been to NDP meetings in the 1980s. I don't think he really was a conservative; I think he was "ideologically flexible", as Stephen Lewis likes to say.

I think his policies were a disaster for this province, but I can still admire his communication skills. He was so much more flamboyant than Getty. His experience as a TV reporter covering Calgary City Hall had taught him how to handle media very well, especially when he was easily recovering from his own scandals.

I now had a very tough new foe, and a big problem. Almost immediately, the media started describing the next election as the "Battle of the Mayors" between Calgary's Klein and Edmonton's Decore. I hadn't been a mayor of anywhere.

Another problem came up when Elections Alberta redrew the electoral map, or rather completely scrambled it. They had been especially unkind with our NDP incumbents, completely changing every one of our urban seats.

In particular, two of our best MLAs, John McInnis and Alex McEachern, had their ridings effectively merged into one redrawn Edmonton-Kingsway. Both of them wanted to run again and both of them wanted to run in their home areas. This started a severe confrontation that wouldn't be resolved until February of 1993.

I stayed out of it as best I could. They were both great MLAs and picking a side would have helped no one. Their robust competition just heaped on more tension to the caucus. Alex won it narrowly.

This was quickly followed by another shock. I was in Calgary speaking at a Rotary Club meeting. As I left the podium, there was a call waiting for me from John McInnis. John said that Stan Woloshyn was about to hold a press conference to announce he was leaving the NDP to become a Progressive Conservative MLA.

I was shocked and angry. Maybe I should have seen it coming, but I hadn't. I knew about the tension between him and Gerry Gibeault, and that his views were a little more small-c conservative than the rest of the caucus. But I'd never dreamed that it would spark Stan into becoming a Tory.

I got back to Edmonton as soon as I could, and the next day I met with Stan. It was a short, tense meeting. We kept our tempers cool. Stan said he was "uncomfortable", and he didn't feel he was a New Democrat. I responded that he had been elected as a New Democrat, and he was obliged to his constituents to finish his term as one.

But it was already a done deal. To this day, I still talk with Stan. I've learned that you have to move on from experiences like this. It's a waste of time to hold grudges. What good does it do you?

I lost another key MLA right after that as well under even more dire circumstances. Pam Barrett had been having a tough time with her health. She had suffered from non-Hodgkin's lymphoma in the 1970s and had a very weak immune system. She definitely didn't have the same energy that she had in her first term as MLA, and Derek Fox and Bob Hawkesworth had even filled in on her House duties.

This opened up the new riding of Edmonton Highlands-Beverly, which we thought would be one of the safer seats for the NDP. John McGinnis quickly announced that he'd run there, and I figured we had solved one problem.

Klein set the next election for June of 1993. In spite of all the ill omens in the previous six months, I actually felt pretty optimistic. I thought our planning had been excellent. I was finally going to be in a real leaders' debate for the first time. We had, in my opinion, the best slate of candidates we'd ever had, including new candidates like Anne McGrath in Calgary or Kay Hurtig in Edmonton Centre.

Most of us in the NDP didn't think Klein or Decore would be good at campaigning. Decore had never been very exciting to watch in the Legislature.

Two things were going wrong on the communications front. One was that the media were stubbornly sticking to the "Battle of the Mayors" narrative, and I was scarcely getting a mention in many stories.

The other problem was a fixation on budget cuts and the deficit. Decore was calling for brutal cuts to government spending, and Klein responded that he would implement "massive cuts". No one wanted to even acknowledge that there might be an alternative to just hacking away at education, health care, and other services people rely on.

I really liked participating in the leaders' debate. I wrote, rehearsed, and felt well prepared to take on Klein and Decore. We did two one-hour debates. I threw everything I could at Klein, who in turned joked that I "didn't attack Decore enough." Many media outlets said that I "won" the debate, and I was thrilled.

Obviously, it didn't matter. Despite my debate, and whatever I did or said after that, we kept dropping. By the time we finally reached election night, I was hoping the NDP would win any seat.

It would be an understatement to say that it was a very different feeling from 1986. After the polls closed, it didn't take long to see that we weren't going to win a single riding. I was beaten in Edmonton-Norwood by someone named Andrew Beniuk. No one could actually remember him doing any campaigning. He had largely gotten his votes from the new neighbourhoods that had been lumped in with Norwood.

Was there something I could have done or said? I don't know.

During the campaign, I never had a conversation with anyone about how bad the polls were looking. Maybe I should have initiated one.

I suppose I could have ordered that some riding campaigns be "collapsed" and sent everyone to Edmonton-Strathcona and Edmonton-Norwood, our seats where we came closest. But we still lost both of them by ten points or more. I doubt it would have changed much.

I think we badly misjudged the impact of Decore's dull performance in the Legislature. We forget sometimes that the vast majority of the population don't watch what happens in that chamber.

I've heard it said that some of our caucus became too preoccupied with the Legislature and didn't concern themselves with their own riding work. It's impossible for me to know what goes on in 16 ridings, but I don't think that's true. I think it would be hard to beat someone like Derek Fox for the outreach work he did in his riding. Besides, there were plenty of PCs in that election who practically ignored their own ridings and yet still survived.

When an election really goes sideways, sometimes it doesn't matter what you do.

I walked out of the victory party convinced that the Alberta NDP would rebuild. But I had no idea how hard it would be.

Part 7: East Edmonton

I decided that I needed to resign the NDP leadership quickly. Hanging on to leadership wouldn't do the party any good after going through a beating like that.

The media decided that the obliteration of my political career was a fascinating story, and were camped out in front of my house for a few days. Cheryl chased them off a couple of times. A friend of ours loaned their cabin to Cheryl and me for a weekend, so we got away from the bedlam for a few days.

I was 52 years old, and I had to decide what I was going to do for a job. I had decided that I definitely wasn't going to be a candidate or politician again. However, they don't give Senate appointments or patronage jobs to old NDP Leaders.

Returning to teaching was definitely out. I hadn't been in a classroom in eleven years, and I was too out of touch on changes to educational methods to step back in. Cheryl had an income from her law career, and we didn't have debts, but I still had to work.

And then, three weeks after Election Day, Premier Klein called me in to meet with him. It was casual. He asked me what I was going to do next. He may have hinted at a government job, but there certainly wasn't any offer. Even if there had been, I didn't want to go down that path. It would've embarrassed the NDP and ruined my credibility.

I was met by a large media scrum coming out of that meeting. Journalists asked me repeatedly if I had been offered a job, and I was honestly able to answer "No." Klein apparently just said that I "had a lot of skills." We didn't meet on it again.

A couple of months after that, I got a call from Investors Group. They asked me to join their staff. They knew I had a lot of contacts from my days in politics, and they were hoping I could sell life insurance and mutual funds to them. I took a required course and actually found it all interesting. The management were very supportive and encouraging. I dived in. Former NDP Staffer Laura Nicholls joined me as a partner.

It was a very different life than the one I had lived as a NDP organizer, MLA, and Leader. I worked a lot of evenings. You had to be available when your clients were. To make a living, you had to have your clients' trust, and after working with them as their MLA, they were willing to trust me. I would get to know what level of risk the client was willing to take on and educate them on just what they were risking.

Some thought that this was an odd or hypocritical job for a social democrat. But I certainly don't think so. I'm not a communist. I believe in the role of the private sector in the economy. But I also believe that businesses need to treat their workers fairly and not screw up our environment. After that, go out there and make as much profit as you can.

There was one thing that my new job and my old job had in common. Everywhere I went, people wanted to talk politics. And while the NDP wasn't my job anymore, it didn't stop the party from looming large in my life.

Almost as soon as I resigned, the party gave me my NDP lifetime membership, which I found ironic. I used to award these to activists that were much older than I was and had done so just a couple of months previously.

All that was left among New Democrat politicians in Alberta was my former staffer, Ross Harvey. That fall, he was up for re-election as Member of Parliament for Edmonton East. As soon as I had gotten out of that awful provincial election, I knew that we had to rally around Ross and save his seat. I pitched in on canvassing, but it didn't come to much. Ross ended up third behind Liberal Judy Bethel. And that was it for Alberta New Democrats in the Legislature and the House of Commons.

As soon as the debacle of the 1993 Federal election was over (the NDP across Canada went from 44 seats to nine), I joined a number of other New Democrats in encouraging Ross to run to replace me as leader of the Alberta NDP.

Ross wasn't terribly enthusiastic at first, but we soon won his interest. His careers as a NDP staffer and M.P. got him name recognition, if nothing else. None of the other former provincial caucus members wanted to take it on. In February of 1994, Ross easily beat three other challengers and won a really tough job.

In early 1994, I think I might've been pretty envious of Laurence Decore's position. The NDP lost 13 of our 16 seats to Liberals in 1993 and he deserves the credit for knocking us from our peak. He won 32 seats in '93 and was now promoted to my old job as Leader of the Official Opposition.

But Decore apparently wasn't happy. I think losing the Premier's seat to Klein affected him more than being shut out of the Legislature affected me. He was used to being the mayor and being in charge. Second place and Opposition Leader was pretty uncomfortable for him. And so, he resigned just a few months after I did.

Every now and then, someone will suggest to me that the NDP and Liberals should "join up" in some fashion because both parties are "progressive". Having seen Decore's lasting impact on Alberta up close, I resent these suggestions. Here's why:

I think Laurence Decore was really the one who reshaped Alberta, not Klein. It was Decore – not Klein – who changed the dialogue around how we governed Alberta for twenty years. He whipped this province up into a hysteria about cutting education, health, and anything else the provincial government could get its hands on. Klein may have carried it out, but Decore was talking about cuts well before Klein showed up.

I think the only reason Decore missed the premier's chair is because he didn't come close to Klein in terms of talent in communicating through the media and directly to Albertans.

Nonetheless, you can see how the Alberta Liberals have suffered in Decore's absence. They've had six leaders in 19 years. They've dropped from 32 seats to one. They are just clinging to life now.

In the 2011 federal election, there was a Conservative candidate by the name of Ryan Hastman who claimed to be the ideological heir to Laurence Decore, and apparently, he took a lot of heat for that statement. I certainly don't think he was the politician that Decore was, but I don't think Hastman was that far off the mark. I think anyone who calls themselves a small-c conservative in Alberta can claim to have the same values as Laurence Decore.

That punishing year of 1993 also delivered another victim in the federal NDP. Audrey McLaughlin stepped down as federal leader in 1994 to no one's surprise. For the first time in a long time, I decided to openly support a leadership candidate in Lorne Nystrom. Lorne had visited Alberta quite a bit while I was leader.

I thought he would be able to show Western Canada that we were ready to support the west better than the Reform party, which now dominated that region. They had won 51 seats in Western Canada and one other in Ontario.

I chose Lorne over Svend Robinson who was perceived, rightly or wrongly, as being too left-wing for most Canadians. My Nova Scotian friend from the early 1980s, Alexa McDonough, was running as well.

I went to that convention in Ottawa in 1995. Lorne came a close third, behind Svend and Alexa. I give Svend Robinson a lot of credit for having the grace to step down and not force a second round of voting. I came out of that convention confident that Alexa would at least improve on the federal NDP's 1993 results.

Back home, my friend and successor Ross Harvey was having a rough ride. It was tough enough leading a party with no seats, but that party was already rebelling against his leadership. Barely a year in, and he was already facing a leadership challenge in November of 1995.

In those days, a NDP leader had to run for their leadership every year. But once you won it once, you'd usually get acclaimed until you stepped down. I had never had a serious challenge in my 11 years as leader.

However, Ross had three people gunning for him, including a very formidable challenge in Anne McGrath, a former unsuccessful star candidate in Calgary (the geographic source of much of Ross's opposition). Nonetheless, Ross beat her and the other two candidates. I think he probably could have carried on through to the 1997 election.

I think Ross was a little more sensitive than a lot of people realize. It was a really tough time for him, as it would have been for anyone. In the space of two years, he had lost a seat in Parliament, took over leadership of a party with no seats, and then confronted a hostile Calgary membership.

I've been a party leader and I can tell you: it's a tough enough job without all of those challenges. Ross resigned shortly after that 1995 convention, and it didn't come as much of a surprise to me. He moved to Vancouver and has a great career there to this day.

We were very lucky to have someone special come back to fill his void. It came as a big shock when Pam Barrett announced that she felt healthy enough to take on the leadership of the Alberta NDP, and she didn't need much of a prodding to run. She steamrolled over three challengers to win it in 1996.

From 1993 on, I had sworn up and down that I was done as an NDP candidate. Through Ross's resignation, I had no thoughts of returning to provincial politics. But I still had the bug. Alexa McDonough was encouraging me to run under her leadership for the federal NDP, and Cheryl wanted me to do it as well. I decided I would run in the next federal election in Edmonton North, just as 1996 turned into 1997.

But before I was able to jump back into being a candidate, Klein called a snap provincial election in Alberta for March of 1997. I definitely wasn't running. I was already committed to running for M.P. and I had no interest in rehashing being an MLA. But I certainly wanted to see Pam and the Alberta NDP succeed.

Former City Councilor Sherry McKibben ran in my old seat of Edmonton Norwood, and I went out to knock on doors for her. But I didn't think we'd win any other seat besides Pam's neighbouring riding of Edmonton Highlands. After a brutal election like 1993, I didn't dream of anything beyond that.

A sociology professor named Dr. Raj Pannu squeaked in by the narrowest of margins in Edmonton Strathcona. New Democrats everywhere were thrilled to get two seats, even as Klein won with 62.

With that out of the way, I could start my own comeback. I was running in a Liberal seat won by John Loney, but he decided not to run again. Deborah Gray, Canada's first Reform M.P., decided to run against me when her riding of Beaver River was dissolved.

I will admit it: I had underestimated the Reform Party before and I did it again with Deborah Gray. Going in, I would have guessed the NDP were tied in Edmonton North with Reform and the Liberals. I was way off the mark.

Of all the election campaigns I was a candidate in, this was my most miserable. While I opposed the conservatism that Lougheed and Getty practiced, I absolutely loathe hateful U.S. style Tea Party conservatism. They use rude, disruptive tactics, and politicians like Gray and Stephen Harper were just fine with profiteering on it well before the term was coined. It makes me sick.

It came to a head at an all-candidates forum at a home for seniors. I found it packed with Reform Party hacks. There were barely any of those seniors to be found, just angry white male Reform partisans.

The moderator quickly lost all control over the room, and it disintegrated into the worst-run all-candidates meeting I've ever seen before or since. The bedlam finally died down, and I left with the two friends that had braved it out with me. But one of the older Reform partisans chased me out.

He screamed at me: "The NDP are for the gays, aren't they?"

It was the last straw for me. I lost my temper, turned, and yelled back into his face: "What's your problem? I know! You're worried about your own sexuality, aren't you?" He looked like he was going to have a heart attack.

I admit it. I'd always wanted to do that to a homophobe. I didn't care that I had said something that was impolitic, to say the least. The behaviour from Gray and her party was so ugly; I was done with being polite to them.

I wound up third with just 17%. I was disappointed. But that disappointment wasn't anywhere near as bad as 1993.

Shortly after that election, I got an interesting proposal from Paul Stanway, editor of the Edmonton Sun. Sun newspapers are probably Canada's most conservative newspaper chains. At that time, they at least wanted to get one progressive view in their editorial section.

I got offered the opportunity to write once a week on provincial politics. For $150 a column, I'd bang out a column on my views on provincial politics, and Cheryl would edit them for me. They also got picked up by the Red Deer Advocate. I enjoyed the opportunity to voice my opinions on Alberta politics.

The next year, Cheryl and I decided we needed a break from it all. I was ready to take a break at work and Cheryl toned down her law practice. We bought a camper van and just hit the road for seven months, skipping the Edmonton winter.

We drove from Saskatchewan to the Florida Keys to Mazatlán in Mexico back to Edmonton, making a lot of stops in between and jumping on a cruise to the Bahamas midway as well. I scanned Alberta news over the internet and kept up with my newspaper columns. I liked Mazatlán so much that Cheryl and I would buy a condo there in 2003.

When I got back, I decided that I was set to run again for Member of Parliament. Edmonton got a lot of visits from Alexa McDonough and it didn't take much convincing to make me want to give it another try in a riding closer to home in Edmonton Centre-East.

I had also noticed how well our new NDP MLAs were doing in the provincial legislature. Pam Barrett's fight on behalf of Albertans who had been a target of a eugenics program sponsored by the provincial government was especially inspiring.

But for all of that, Pam was going through some tough times personally. It culminated one day in 2000 on a dentist's chair where she had an allergic reaction to anesthetic. She had a "near-death experience." She decided it was grounds to remove herself from politics.

The Alberta NDP was going to face yet another must-win by-election in Edmonton Highlands. Although I had already broken my vow of never being a candidate again, I still didn't want to rehash the Alberta Legislature. I was still more interested in running for the House of Commons again, so there was no talk of running myself in the by-election.

Rather, I wanted to see Brian Mason run in Pam's place. The local city councilor who I had helped out in 1989 had won re-election three times since. I joined a large group of people who bugged him into running. He said "no" a lot of times, and then caved in at the very last minute. I still don't understand what changed his mind, but I'm glad he did. He won the nomination easily and swept the by-election with ease.

When the 2000 federal election came, I quit my column and dived into challenging Peter Goldring in Edmonton East. I had a bigger campaign with a bigger budget than in 1997, but it turned out to be a grim election for the NDP, and the party lost several seats. Edmonton East was one of the few places where the NDP improved, from 12% to 17%. I was disappointed again, but I was starting to get used to it. Maybe I was just punch-drunk.

And soon after that, the provincial NDP were faced with another tough election in early 2001. Raj Pannu had taken over leadership of the provincial party after Pam.

Dr. Raj Pannu is the sort of person that, when you meet him, you're inevitably impressed by him. I was pretty optimistic about his chances as leader. He talked to me and others about his concern about his age (he was 67 at that point).

My advice to him was to not talk about it. No one would care if he didn't draw attention to it. I went out and door knocked in Norwood again, this time for housing activist Harvey Voogd.

At that time, a rock/rap band called "Rage Against the Machine" was pretty popular. Some clever person started putting out t-shirts in that election with "Raj Against the Machine" across the chest. I thought they were hilarious. But I don't think poor Raj got the joke until someone explained it after the election. The shirts were in heavy demand very quickly. Good luck finding one today; they're a collector's item.

Raj had the bad luck to be up against Klein at his most popular and most effective. We only kept Raj and Brian Mason in that election and felt pretty lucky to have achieved that. Klein swept 74 out of 83 seats. Nancy MacBeth (nee Betkowski) had jumped ship to the Liberals and got soundly out-communicated by Klein, just like Decore and Mitchell before her.

At that point, I stepped down from Investors Group. After seven years, I had developed enough of a client base that demanded a lot of my attention, and I had to decide if that was all I wanted to do for the rest of my life. I had other interests that I wanted to pursue.

One was just down the road from me. Alex Taylor School was an important inner-city school in Norwood. It was one of many schools that were trying to keep these tough neighbourhoods vibrant and alive. But the Edmonton Public School Board was intent on shutting it down, along with several others like it.

This was craziness. Any attempt at urban renewal is pointless if you don't have a healthy public school in a neighbourhood. A young family isn't going to move into a neighbourhood without a good school. School closures just lead to urban sprawl, as those families wind up migrating to suburbs on the edge of town. And the elementary school students suffer the most when they're packed into giant schools and classes. Anyone who's studied the issue will tell you that. Being a former teacher myself, I was pretty angry about how this Norwood school was being treated.

My campaign manager from the 2000 election, Berend Wilting, along with unions who represented school board workers, suggested to me that I should run for the school board. By the end of the summer of 2001, I was hooked on the idea. I ran in the ward that I lived in. It included the better part of my old riding of Norwood, as well as Beverly, Highlands, Newton, and others. These were the neighbourhoods most deeply affected by the board's school closures.

I was challenging an incumbent in Terry Sulyma who had supported the school closures. Terry didn't do all that much to defend himself. The campaigning for school board was a lot less intense than provincial or federal elections. I just door-knocked and volunteers put up signs. Name recognition was a lot more crucial though, which I had from my time as MLA and party leader. There was only one very small all-candidates' meeting sponsored by the board.

I went into election night feeling pretty confident and walked out with 66% of the vote. After three losses, I was reminded that winning was a lot more fun than losing.

I really liked being a school board trustee. It's very different from being an MLA. You're one independent out of a group of just nine. It's meant to be a part-time job, but I treated it like a full-time position and put in extra time touring schools and keeping in touch with school principals. I also got to speak to school graduations, which was an uplifting experience every time.

I had a big problem with a lot of the other board members. Most of them were former school administrators. They were under the impression that they "weren't politicians" and that they still could behave like administrators instead of representatives of the people that lived in their ward.

I tried to set them straight:" You ran in an election, didn't you? You represent those people, not the administration." How these people thought they were somehow able to behave as bureaucrats and school principals still bewilders me to this day.

My best guess is there were too many trustees getting seats because no one would run against them. They were older than you might think too. I was one of the younger trustees at 60. One of the better trustees was a familiar face: Gerry Gibeault, one of the former NDP MLAs from the glory days.

Besides the threat of school closures, the provincial government was still looking for ways to strip money out of education. Klein and

Education Minister Lyle Oberg decided to push the board into a strike by withdrawing money for teachers' salaries.

Believe it or not, I was on the negotiating committee for Board management. It was a bit of an odd place for a politician who supported, and had been supported by, the labour movement. Nonetheless, I was happy to be in that position. I believe in the necessity of collective bargaining, which means someone has to sit at the management end. I don't think collective bargaining has to be adversarial either. Eventually, we came to an agreement that put the students first.

In doing so, the school board trustees now had to go to PC Education Minister Lyle Oberg for funding. Oberg was a real piece of work. Instead of providing my board and others with the funds to meet our students' needs, he accused us of financial mismanagement. He even set up a probe of our board to scare up evidence of our "mismanagement". It came to nothing, of course.

Why would he pull a stunt like this? I think there are two reasons: The PC fiscal priority was — and is — to pour as much resources into oil companies in the form of tax breaks and royalty breaks. In the mind of PCs like Oberg, if that means that a few Edmonton schools don't have enough teachers, then so be it.

The second reason is that this Tory crew had run the province for 31 years at that point and had become petty and arrogant, especially in the face of some school board trustees trying to get them to pay for teachers.

After the "probe" cleared us, we met with Oberg again, and he was a lot friendlier. But this Tory attitude is still a problem to this day.

During my time on the school board, the NDP took a back seat to my trustee duties, but I didn't completely ignore my party. In 2002, Alexa resigned her leadership after that tough 2000 election. I like Alexa very much, and I think she's a big reason that the Nova Scotia NDP would go on to win government in 2009, but she picked the right time to go.

I quickly decided that I would support Bill Blaikie, the NDP MP for Winnipeg-Transcona, and a former United Church minister. I wanted someone who would resonate with east Edmonton voters. When Bill's on a roll, he can give amazing speeches, including an amazing one at the 2001 convention in Winnipeg. He had served as health critic and done a great job.

Yes, I had supported Lorne Nystrom just seven years earlier, but I didn't get the sense that he was going to be able to launch as strong a campaign as he had in 1995 (which had only been good enough for third place).

I found some time to do a little bit of organizing for Bill. I made some phone calls to members to talk them into voting for him. I went to the convention in Toronto to talk to delegates who hadn't voted yet as well.

Bill Blaikie started out as the front-runner in that race, but he definitely didn't stay that way. A Toronto city councilor that I'd never met before had started making a name for himself with New Democrats in Edmonton and across the country. He went by the name of Jack Layton.

I didn't have a clue who he was, but Brian Mason was pretty enthusiastic about him. They were friends from when they were both involved in the Federation of Canadian Municipalities in the 1990s. From what little I saw of him in that campaign, I joined the ranks of those who said he was way too slick to appeal to NDP voters, especially voters in Edmonton.

When I wound up at the 2003 Toronto convention to support Bill, I knew it was down to him and Jack. Jack won easily on the first ballot.

I was disappointed. For all the confidence that Brian Mason and others had in him, I sure didn't have much. But I'm a team player and I got behind him when election time came again.

At the school board, I continued to work on the issue that had driven me to run to be a school board trustee: preventing school closures in the inner-city neighbourhoods of Edmonton. In 2003, the issue finally came to a head. On one side were a group of trustees who had a similar view as me. On the other were a school board bureaucracy and superintendent who were intent on shutting down schools.

The trick the bureaucracy pulled was the process they devised to assess how necessary each school was. Instead of looking at each school individually, they would assess them in groups, and then decide which group needed less schools, and then arbitrarily axe them. This process was brought for a vote amongst trustees.

Many on the board were nervous about bucking the school bureaucracy. Remember, a lot of these trustees thought of themselves more as bureaucrats than elected representatives. A fellow trustee named Bill Bonko and I spent a lot of time on the phone with other trustees trying to talk them into doing the right thing. In the end, we got the votes we needed.

This earned me a call from the superintendent, looking to compromise far too late. "How can we fix this?" he asked.

"You can't." I replied. "It's done."

That moment is still a highlight for me in all my years in politics.

In early 2004, I had a decision to make on my future. My term on the school board was coming to a close, and I didn't know what to do about it.

My former business partner, Laura Nicholls, was now the provincial secretary of the Alberta NDP, running day-to-day party operations just as I had done in the 1970s. She began talking to me about Edmonton Beverly-Clareview, a riding in Edmonton's northeast, and their need for a quality candidate.

This, of course, had been NDP MLA Ed Ewasiuk's seat from 1986 to 1993. The NDP had almost won it back in 1997. It was a whole new neighbourhood to me; it had no overlap with the Edmonton-Norwood riding I had represented and had since been dissolved.

Laura was pretty persuasive, and Cheryl was enthusiastic and supportive, just like every other time I ran for anything. I felt I still had something to offer Alberta, and it was about time that the Alberta NDP won a third seat. I decided it was time to get back in the provincial arena.

I was nominated in the late spring and once again, I got Dave Barrett to speak to my nomination meeting, almost thirty years from the first time he had done this for me. The riding association had gone dormant, so I had to be a little more hands-on in building a campaign than I usually am. I'm usually happy to leave it to activists and a campaign manager and go knock on doors, but that wasn't an option for the first few months.

A federal election came in June of 2004. Jack Layton called me to ask me to run again, but I was already committed to running provincially and was hard at work on that.

We had a change of leadership in the Alberta NDP in September of 2004. Brian Mason was acclaimed to take over for Raj Pannu. This wasn't a surprise; it'd been in the works for a while. Raj was set to run again for MLA, but just didn't want leadership anymore, and Brian was many years younger.

It was good news for my run in Beverly-Clareview, as Brian had represented those neighbourhoods on council. The election was called by Ralph Klein for November. I was given a veteran campaign manager named Brian Nixon to manage my campaign, so I could finally just stick to door knocking.

I was running against a three-term MLA named Julius Yankowsky. Or, at least I think I was. I never saw the guy, except at one all-candidates' meeting. He had been elected as a Liberal in 1993, crossed the floor to the PCs in 1994, and hadn't done a lot since then.

It was an interesting election for me, as PC blowouts go, for several reasons. Edmonton will sometimes swing from opposition to PC and back every election. After the Liberals and NDP getting hammered in 2001, the pendulum swung back. Unfortunately, this only tended to happen in Edmonton. The rest of the province seemed immune to this.

Ralph Klein and "massive cuts" were wearing thin in Edmonton and the consequences were starting to show in Edmonton Beverly-Clareview as I went door-to-door. Yankowsky was invisible right to the end, and voters still remembered me from my days as NDP Leader.

I spent election night in the campaign office. I was fifteen years removed from my last win as an MLA, and I got a reminder about how good it feels to be one again. And it was a decisive win, sweeping every neighbourhood in the riding for 51% - much more than I had expected.

I had another pleasant surprise when I joined the victory party in downtown Edmonton. Brian Mason and Raj Pannu had easily won their seats, and we had won a fourth seat: David Eggen in Edmonton Calder. For the first time since we had lost everything in 1993, we had regained the status of a recognized party in the Legislature.

It was surprisingly easy to return to MLA life. Legislature debates and constituency work remained reflex for me. I didn't miss being leader, but I missed getting the first question in Question Period. Brian Mason handled that privilege of leadership well, so at least I never felt it was wasted.

Brian had one curveball to throw at me. He made me House Leader for the NDP caucus. I had served for a short time as House Leader from 1982 to 1984, but I hadn't really dived into that job then.

House Leader is a job with a lot of unheralded tasks, including being the MLA who's well-versed in Legislative procedure. You have to learn complicated old tomes of rules like "Beauchesne's Parliamentary Rules and Forms" or "Erskine & May: Parliamentary Practice".

You're supposed to know all this procedure to nail the government when they bend the rules and defend the members of your own caucus when they get accused of making trouble. I admit it bores the crap out of me, and I never really wrapped my head around much of it. It didn't take long for me to get caught out on my lack of study.

Early on in 2005, Brian Mason said something to rile up the Tories. They started the usual accusations of unparliamentary behaviour and language. For all I knew, they may have been right. Brian loves being provocative and getting under the skin of conservatives. Within minutes, a fairly irritated Speaker Ken Kowalski called on me to give Brian's defense.

I stood up and gave the only defense I could think of. "Mr. Speaker ... What are you gonna do?" I shrugged and sat down. If nothing else, it got laughs.

Not every facet of Legislature culture was familiar to me. It was a completely new set of caucus mates from the generation I had served with previously.

I really liked working with all three of them. Brian Mason had been a friend for years. He always handled the duties of leadership in the Legislature very well. He had a tougher time of it than I did, leading a caucus of four instead of sixteen.

Raj Pannu had won a massive victory in Edmonton Strathcona at the age of 70, but he was definitely set to make it his last term. He would still do his work in the Legislature and in his riding, but he wasn't touring the province very much.

The real new guy for me was a young teacher named David Eggen. Dave had won Christine Mjolness' old riding of Edmonton Calder in a very narrow upset over PC MLA Brent Rathgeber. He had talked to me a couple of times before the election about being a candidate.

He turned out to be a real keener. He worked hard and really wanted to learn, and he and I wound up spending a lot of time in the Legislature. He's called me a "mentor" since, which I appreciate.

The other big adjustment I had was in the Legislature itself. In my first 11 years, we would be tough on the PCs and they'd be tough on us, but we would still treat each other like human beings. When we stepped away from the microphone, we could get along and behave like grown-ups. I was actually close friends with some of them, like PC cabinet minister Dick Johnson.

I saw that atmosphere had died in my absence. I got to see an example of the new normal in the Legislature very quickly.

"Pages" are young students that are brought in to assist in a Legislature chamber. In Alberta, they're very young, just 15 or 16 years old. One afternoon, I was sitting through a Liberal MLA's speech on health care, and for emphasis, they sent a copy of their health care platform to Ralph Klein, carried by a young page. Ralph responded by calling the document "garbage" and hurling it at the page.

Think about that for a second. He hurled a book at a teenage kid for no reason other than that he was a little irritated. It cheapened him, and it cheapened the Legislature as far as I'm concerned.

And he got away with it. Ralph Klein did stupid stuff like that all the time. He would respond with a somewhat contrite apology, and all would be forgiven. I don't know another politician who could pull it off as easily and as frequently as he did.

Another was his response to the "mad cow" disease crisis. At that time, Alberta cattle were being struck by "Bovine Spongiform

Encephalopathy", or more popularly, "Mad Cow Disease." Alberta's beef exports were being closed down at borders around the world. Alberta's cattle ranchers took a big financial hit.

Instead of taking action to clean up our beef industry, restore our reputation, and provide help to cattle farmers, Klein publicly called on farmers to cover it up. "Shoot, shovel, and shut up" is what he actually said. The PCs have never learned how to handle a crisis like this. Their other venture was to start an "I love Alberta Beef" bumper sticker campaign. It did improve morale, but not much else, and cattle ranchers continued to suffer for years after.

Another example came all the way from Fort McMurray. I would up meeting some developers who claimed that they had been trying to apply for contracts from the provincial government. Fort McMurray had a lot of construction happening. They hadn't had much success, and felt that the process was unfair, possibly even rigged.

We had our caucus researchers look up which developers did win those contracts. And then we looked up the list of donors to the PC MLA for Fort McMurray, Guy Boutilier, who was also a cabinet minister. We saw a lot of the same names in both lists.

I did a press conference to let Albertans know what we'd found. The PCs must have gotten wind of it while I was talking to the media. Half way through, Guy Boutilier walks in and sits down right in front of me.

If the media had been bored by my remarks thus far, they sure were interested now. Very soon, Boutilier stood up and interrupted me. He started rambling that I was "hurting his family". I let him go on for a bit, and then cut him off. "That's enough, this is our news conference. It's over." He continued to rant as he went out the door, and I told him that if he was going to be in politics, he'd need to develop a thicker skin.

Finally, the media had changed as well. A good example was Dave Rutherford, who is a big name in radio in Alberta. He was the veteran late-morning host on CHQR in Calgary for decades, and his show was picked up by stations around the province. I was on there often as NDP leader in the 80s and early 90s.

In those days, Dave took a very moderate tone in both his political editorializing and how he handled guests. He wasn't pro-NDP, but he was pretty even handed.

When I returned to the Legislature, Dave had really changed. He would deliver hardline radical conservative rants, cut off guests he disagreed with, and behave like a bully. I guess he had embraced the Rush Limbaugh style of crazy right-wing radio. To this day, I don't know if that is how he really thinks or if he was just putting on an act to get attention.

After losing seats in 2004, Klein was starting to fall out of favour with his own party. Lyle Oberg, the former education minister, was kicked out of caucus after disavowing him at a meeting of his riding association. In March of 2006, only 55% of PC Convention delegates voted to support Klein's leadership. He didn't technically have to quit, but in reality, he didn't have the needed support. I was pretty surprised to see his party turn on him in such numbers.

I'm sure it must have surprised and hurt Klein a lot as well. Coming out of that fateful 1993 election, I think he saw himself as something of a messiah for the PC party, and he had delivered three more overwhelming victories for his party since then.

He announced he would resign, but not quickly. He vowed to stay on until December of 2006.

There were eight candidates to replace Klein in the end, but only three of them were competitive. Jim Dinning was who we, and most other people, were expecting to win. That was certainly who we were preparing to campaign against.

I knew Dinning from his days as a Getty-era cabinet minister. After quitting in 1997, he came back from corporate Calgary to run for premier. Most of the pre-election planning that we did in the summer and fall of 2006 was done on the assumption that Dinning would win the leadership in November.

Ted Morton was a former political science professor from the University of Calgary. He was a member of the "Calgary School" of hardline conservatism that had fueled the Reform Party, the Klein government, the Harper government, and a lot of other hardline conservative governments across Canada. He had run in a safe PC seat in the 2004 election. and was pretty open about his motivations: Even Ralph Klein wasn't conservative enough for Ted, and he was intent on fixing that by becoming the next premier. He had already made waves by tabling an anti-gay private member's bill that we had filibustered against in 2006.

I actually had gotten to know him pretty well. He sat right across the aisle from me and we'd have fun heckling each other. I think his politics are contemptible, but I got along with him.

No one gave Ed Stelmach a lot of attention. He wasn't divisive and controversial like Ted Morton. He didn't have a $2 million campaign budget and wasn't perceived as a front-runner like Jim Dinning. In fact, I had never even heard Ed Stelmach speak in the Legislature during that term, prior to his announcement that he would quit his position as Intergovernmental Affairs Minister to run for Leader. He'd been an MLA since 1993, when he beat our NDP incumbent, Derek Fox.

With the PC's odd leadership voting system, Dinning, Morton, and Stelmach were left for the final ballot. And that's when Stelmach's campaign started to take off. PCs like to stay loyal to their region, and Stelmach had Edmonton and rural Alberta ostensibly to himself and left Calgary and right-wing purists to Dinning and Morton. Sure enough, on the second ballot, Ed Stelmach narrowly won the PC leadership and the Premier's chair.

This was worrying to me personally in Edmonton Beverly-Clareview. A Calgary corporate executive like Dining or an ideologue like Morton wouldn't have enthralled many voters in my riding. But a Ukrainian farmer who had worked his way up to Premier certainly would.

Ukrainians in Alberta have not had an easy history. They were slapped with the epithet of "DPs" (short for displaced persons), and were discriminated against in business, government offices and workplaces. A lot of the working-class Ukrainian families who had been hit hard by that kind of prejudice lived in Beverly.

I can't blame these folks for being excited at the prospect of a Ukrainian premier. The same thing had happened with the Saskatchewan Ukrainian community when Roy Romanow became Premier. When I started canvassing again after Stelmach's win, I was still welcomed warmly in Ukrainian households, but I was still perturbed.

As for Stelmach, I think he was surprised to have wound up as Premier. For the year and a half that I watched his Premiership up close, I think he wanted to be the sort of conservative that Peter Lougheed was. He had talked about getting more value from the meagre royalties that Alberta collects off the oil sands, or putting the brakes on raw bitumen exports and staring to build refining capacity in Alberta. But that's not what happened.

I had a special challenge come up in early 2007. Alberta was going through another economic boom, but not a lot of Albertans were feeling the benefits. One group who were particularly affected were renters.

Alberta had very few rules governing rent and rent increases. Lots of housing was being built, but very little of it was affordable for a normal working family.

I wound up being the point person on this issue for the caucus, and I was happy to take on this project in the Legislature and in front of the media. After the issue had been kicked around in the Legislature and a lot of horror stories of massive rent hikes landed in the media, Stelmach had to allow for some new ideas.

The PCs set up a committee to tour and hold hearings into the housing crisis. It was chaired by Calgary PC MLA Len Webber, who did a very good job, and included MLAs and stakeholder groups as well. And one spot was left for the NDP. Brian Mason tapped me to sit on the committee and hit the road for hearings.

We heard from a very wide cross-section of people involved in housing Albertans in any event. We certainly heard from plenty of corporate landlords. We heard that old argument that if we restricted increases in rent in any way, there would be no new housing built.

But there was hardly any affordable housing being built in most Alberta communities. In fact, what was happening more often than not was that landlords were turning apartments into very expensive condominiums, booting out the tenants, and trying to sell the units off.

But we heard from more pragmatic housing advocates, municipal elected officials, and tenants. And in the end, the majority of the committee outvoted the PC's supported proposed rent guidelines that would have put the brakes on out-of-control rent hikes and condo conversions. They went in the committee's report ...

... And were promptly thrown out by Stelmach and the PCs. They refused to get past their stubborn ideology that compelled them to believe that the market was always right, no matter how many pensioners or working families got kicked out to the street. It was a disappointment to me, and even more so to the renters, but not a surprise. The PCs adopted a few half-hearted measures from the report and claimed they had fixed the problem.

At this point, I returned to prepping myself for re-election. I had a new motivation to get back to canvassing. Grant Notley's daughter, Rachel Notley, had been nominated to run in Raj Pannu's seat of Edmonton Strathcona.

Rachel had gone on to work for a time at the NDP caucus while I was leader. She then became a labour lawyer, worked for the BC NDP government in the 1990s, and finally had come back to work for the United Nurses of Alberta.

When Raj announced his resignation, Rachel had launched an impressive nomination campaign that attracted no challengers. Needless to say, Rachel is a formidable candidate in her own right. However, I really liked the idea of being able to potentially work alongside two generations of Notleys in the Legislature.

As worried as I was, canvassing in the fall of 2007 continued to go very well. I remember canvassing the Beacon Heights neighbourhood in Beverly one evening and getting requests for signs all over the place.

The PCs had a tough time even finding someone to run against me. Tony Vandermeer had been a PC MLA for neighbouring Edmonton-Manning from 2001 to 2004 but had lost his seat in that election. He had tried to regain the Edmonton-Manning PC nomination in 2008 but had lost that too.

Someone must have talked him into running against me, because he was promptly nominated after that. But I wasn't terribly worried about him. I was worried about Stelmach and the Ukrainian voters.

In January of 2008, the Building Trades Unions of Alberta and the Alberta Federation of Labour launched a "third party" campaign of advertising against Ed Stelmach. It was a set of cheesily-produced attack ads that claimed he had "no plan", even though he very easily produced one in response. These expensive ads created a lot of sympathy for Stelmach.

These labour groups could have spent their members' money a lot of better ways, politically. Even if they had chucked them at the Liberals as well as NDP candidates, it probably would have been more effective. I'm glad they learned their lesson and didn't repeat the exercise in 2012.

In early February, the election call came. It'll come to no one's surprise that Alberta's weather was absolutely brutal that winter, and it was no accident that the PCs picked that time to have an election. It's an old trick that Lougheed used all the time. Making it difficult to canvass means that most people's exposure to candidates comes through advertising, or the "air war."

There's only one party that can really saturate the airwaves, and that's the PCs. A bad weather election gives them a real advantage. The Liberals had a lot of hype from a few media outlets, but in Beverly-Clareview, we didn't see much evidence of any burgeoning Liberal support. In fact, throughout much of the campaign I thought we might have picked up a couple of seats in Edmonton.

For me, it was a very sedate campaign of just plodding through the snow from door to door. Brian Mason visited our campaign a few times. Former BC NDP Premier Dave Barrett visited my campaign too, making it four decades of visits by Barrett to my campaigns. Unfortunately, it'd be his last.

Finally, we had one more Election Day of miserable weather and knocking on doors to try and convince them to vote in the thick, slushy snow. I finally got in to watch the results, which turned out to be as miserable as the weather. I went from 51% to 36% and fell below PC Tony Vandermeer. Even in Beacon Heights, where I had gotten such a warm welcome, I only tied Vandermeer. My foreboding about losing the Ukrainian vote to Stelmach proved correct.

Cheryl was also very disappointed at this loss. She has never been one to mince words and she used some pretty sharp ones that night. "Why would people do this?" she said. "You've been a good MLA!" But I'd been there before. I know that sometimes being a good MLA isn't good enough.

We went to the central victory party. I greeted Dave Eggen who had lost his seat by an even narrower margin. We said a few words from the podium and I walked out of the hall with no idea of what to do next.

I didn't take losing my seat as hard as I had in 1993. Losing your seat is not something you want to be well-practiced at, but I had learned to handle it better now. My young Constituency Assistant, Kris Andreychuk, lost his job as well, but bounced back quickly. I decided to take off to our place in Mazatlán to unwind.

I was 67, but I was in no mood to retire. Cheryl was still working, and I just hate the idea of sitting around doing nothing and waiting to pass away. I felt I still had something to offer Alberta. And hey, there is always another election …

Another federal election was indeed coming. Edmonton East needed an NDP candidate, and it now contained most of Edmonton

Beverly-Clareview and all of Brian Mason's riding. I didn't have to muse aloud in front of very many people before Jack Layton called me.

It's around this time I started to get to know Jack Layton a lot better. He was very enthusiastic when he called and left me his cell number. I have to admit, I didn't hand out my phone number when I was leader like Jack would. I didn't call him a lot, maybe four or five times over the years.

I knew Edmonton East very well, and that it was going to be an uphill struggle. The south end of the riding voted NDP provincially, but the north end hadn't in decades. The incumbent, Peter Goldring, still hadn't put down strong roots in the 11 years since I had last run against him. The NDP riding association didn't have a debt, but it didn't have much of anything else.

I made up my mind to go ahead with it in the spring. Jack and I quickly announced my candidacy in July. Just a few months after finishing canvassing for myself in the provincial election, I was back at it again. I got some comments at the door that Jack Layton was "too slick" for them, just as I had thought in 2003.

But my mind was changed on that, and I thought others would be changed soon too. That criticism drove Cheryl up the wall though, as she had become a very big fan of Jack. I figured I had plenty of time to change everyone's mind before the election in 2009.

Except that election didn't come in 2009. Stephen Harper decided to break his own fixed-election laws and call an election in September of 2008. My campaign manager wasn't thrilled to have been caught by surprise like that, but I'm always happy to see the election get started.

Most Edmonton New Democrats were preoccupied with getting Linda Duncan elected in the neighbouring riding of Edmonton Strathcona. She had come a close second in the 2006 election. Some worried that my campaign would "siphon off" resources from Linda. They thought it could cost her the election.

I think that's ridiculous. Having credible NDP candidates and campaigns across cities like Calgary or Edmonton is only going to help voters to believe that we can win.

The 2008 Federal Election was a little more exciting than the provincial election that I had just finished. Goldring didn't do very much to defend himself; he didn't even attend an all-candidates meeting held at a conservative private university. I got to M.C. a huge NDP rally at the Winspear Centre concert hall. I had a surprising number of old friends and foes come out to support me, including former PC MLA Peter Elzinga and Social Credit MLA Walt Buck.

At the end of the short campaign, we made progress, taking the NDP from 18% to 31% in Edmonton East. We had hardly broached the north end of the riding but made great progress everywhere else. More importantly, Linda Duncan won her seat and became Alberta's second ever NDP Member of Parliament after Ross Harvey.

Another new Member of Parliament who won that night was Don Davies, one of our great staffers from my time as leader. He had been a great researcher, and then moved to Vancouver in 1991. At the time, he was very torn up about having to leave. 17 years later, he was a Member of Parliament in Vancouver. I think he's done a great job since, and I'm very proud to have had him on our Alberta NDP team.

Once again, I walked out of that campaign saying that I was done as a candidate. I told the campaign manager to throw out the lawn signs. Fortunately, he didn't believe me.

My election was done, but the drama in Ottawa had just gotten started. What happened next is well-recorded history now. Jack Layton decided to try to form a minority government with the Liberals, and the country started arguing with itself in the media and in protests. I don't have any great insights on how it came about, and I wasn't privy to any details. I watched it all on the news like everyone else.

What I saw didn't look that good. I'm hardly the first one to say it, but the visual of Jack Layton sitting at the same table as Gillies Duceppe gave birth to the notion that we had somehow let the separatists into government, even though that wasn't the case at all.

The Conservative response to the coalition can only be described as hysterical, especially in Alberta. For starters, calling it "undemocratic" was ludicrous. A government that had only received 37% of the vote doesn't have much of a mandate themselves. There's precedent for coalition governments in every country that uses the Westminster model of Parliament, including Canada.

What was undemocratic was proroguing Parliament and shutting down government just because the Prime Minister wasn't going to get his way. The Lieutenant Governor should have never let him get away with it.

If she had done the right thing, I would have been happy to "come out of retirement" and run again in a snap election. It would have been daunting and I might have gotten clobbered, but I'm not about to walk away from my party just because it's a tough time.

As a former party leader, I might have tried the same thing as Jack had I been placed in his situation. He probably was better suited for that challenge as he had municipal government experience that I didn't have. But it all came to naught, and Harper clung to power

In 2009, I quickly got restless again. I was still healthy. Cheryl was still working for the provincial government and I wasn't working at all.

I still felt like I had something to offer Alberta. We had made great progress in Edmonton East in the 2008 Federal Election in just three months. What if we had a year or two?

The tenuous minority government couldn't last much longer. Every spring and fall, the Harper government seemed to be teetering on losing a non-confidence vote.

In April, I decided that I wanted to have one more crack at Member of Parliament for Edmonton East, and we had a great nomination meeting that July.

It wasn't just for me either. Lewis Cardinal, an educator and aboriginal activist, was running next door in Edmonton Centre. If you've ever heard or met Lewis, he's a very inspiring speaker and individual. He had run for municipal office in 2007, coming within half a percentage point of being a city councilor.

We held this nomination in familiar territory. Cheryl had been president of Alberta Avenue's Community League, right in the heart of Norwood, and ostensibly the geographic centre of my political career. We held a great nomination meeting with Jack, Linda Duncan, and a lot of people from my neighbourhood.

For two years, I hit the pavement, canvassing most of Edmonton East's more conservative north end, with the occasional break in Mazatlán. The reception was better than I was expecting, and I soon became convinced that we really did have a shot at winning.

I also got to know Jack Layton a lot better during this time. He visited Edmonton a lot, and he phoned me fairly often. Much has been said about how he was a special person, and that's where I became convinced of it too. When you're a leader, it's very hard to deal with the many people who want a piece of your time. Somehow Jack made it look effortless.

Cheryl and I took a break over December of 2010 and January 2011 in Mazatlán. It was there that Cheryl became very ill.

At first, we thought it was just a bad case of pneumonia. But when she was examined, we had much worse news – lung cancer. We were told it was treatable, but it wouldn't be easy, and it wouldn't be short.

I was immediately set to quit as a candidate, but I got overruled pretty fast. "You're not quitting." Cheryl said. "I won't be responsible for that."

With that, we returned to Edmonton and Cheryl set on a course of punishing chemotherapy. I tried to canvass and stay focused on my job. It wasn't easy to go back to the campaign, but the doctors told us the treatment was going well, so I was optimistic about Cheryl's progress throughout the treatment.

As I hit the pavement, I started to get a little more pessimistic about the next election, feeling that both the NDP and I would get roughly the same results that we'd gotten in 2008. At the very least, I finished up canvassing the conservative neighbourhoods in the north. I then returned to familiar territory in Norwood and Beverly.

I spent the 2011 campaign largely canvassing and taking Cheryl to appointments. Jack came to Edmonton for two fantastic rallies. This included the legendary first rally of the campaign in Edmonton's new art gallery in March of 2011.

Cheryl was well enough to come with me. We were very moved when Jack, himself a cancer survivor, recognized her in the crowd and wish her well in front of hundreds of supporters.

At some point – it's hard for me to point to when – the campaign turned into the "Orange Wave". The canvassing got better as the days progressed. Obviously, Edmonton East is a long way from Quebec, so I was only nominally aware of what was going on there.

In the last week, that wave caught up to me. We had a massive rally with Jack at Fort Edmonton Park, with thousands in attendance. If I didn't feel it before then, I could definitely feel an orange wave now. As great as the first rally went, you could feel something amazing about to happen.

I talked to Jack briefly at both these events. Even in the face of the challenges, he was upbeat, and focused on encouraging Lewis, Linda, and I. He was focused on us more than being concerned about himself. He was, and in my mind still is, a great motivator.

And in a week, a horde of media suddenly decided that I was the story in the stretch run. I did a ton of interviews on that last weekend. An activist NGO called "Avaaz" sent e-mails to thousands of Canadians saying that Edmonton East was the "key riding" to stop the Harper majority.

That attention brought in dozens of new volunteers and a lot of money, even though it was well past the point at which we could spend any of it. I didn't even know about most of this until my campaign manager told me about it on election night.

As I said, I thought I had a shot at being a Member of Parliament on Election Day. And the 17,000 votes and 37% we did get might have been enough to win in some ridings. But just as Edmonton East caught some of the "Orange Wave", the Harper wave caught my riding too. I still got soundly beaten in the north end of the riding and lost by 15%.

When I walked into the victory party, I saw the results across the rest of Canada. I saw results for my party that I hadn't ever seen in my 70 years. I walked into the hall hoping to see the NDP win 50 seats – maybe five or ten in Quebec. Seeing a big screen TV announce 103 NDP seats was stunning. I never dreamed we'd ever decimate the Liberals like that in my lifetime. Linda was re-elected by a wide margin. Lewis had a very strong second place showing.

Needless to say, it was a bittersweet night. Cheryl and I got up to the podium, thanked an enormous crowd of volunteers, and announced (yet again) that I would never seek public office again. Cheryl and I were ready to walk off into the sunset together.

In April, Cheryl had been doing great. In addition to rallies, she had even spent the last week of the campaign working with volunteers at phone canvassing.

But it wasn't to be. After that election night, Cheryl's recovery took an immediate turn for the worse.

By June, we were told that Cheryl wasn't going to make it. I coped as best as I could, but it was very hard to stay positive. You just don't have a choice when you're in that situation. Our family came together to help quickly. This included Cheryl's sister, a nurse, who moved in to help.

On July 25th, I watched as Jack Layton went to the country to announce that he too had cancer again. Having spent almost six months dealing with Cheryl's cancer, I could tell by how gaunt Jack looked that he was in serious trouble.

On July 29th, Cheryl died in my arms.

It was very difficult after that. Cheryl hadn't made many plans for her death, and in spite of my grief, I had tough decisions to make. The first was her memorial.

Alberta Avenue was her neighbourhood and the community league hall on 118th Avenue was the natural place for a memorial service. A room that usually could hold 150-200 people was packed to the rafters beyond that amount. All of our grandchildren spoke at the service. It was brutal for me at the time, but I'm now able to look back on it with a lot of warmth.

After the service, my Blackberry buzzed with a message. Surprisingly, it was from Jack Layton:

JACK LAYTON, MP, DÉPUTÉ
TORONTO - DANFORTH
LEADER, NEW DEMOCRATIC PARTY
CHEF, NOUVEAU PARTI DÉMOCRATIQUE

August 03, 2011

Ray Martin
704-8220 Jasper Avenue NW
Edmonton, Alberta
T5H 4B6

Dear Ray:

Please accept this letter as an expression of my deepest sympathy to you and your entire family at the passing of Cheryl.

Cheryl's political legacy and tireless work to advance the goals of the social democratic movement will live on, continuing to affect the lives of Albertans and Canadian families from coast to coast to coast. New Democrats are forever thankful to Cheryl for her dedication and leadership in reminding us all of the importance of improving the communities in which we live.

More than that, I'm sure you, Barrett, Cathy, Matthew, Bruce, Dawn, and all of your grandchildren will remember Cheryl as the loving wife, mother and grandmother I know she was.

My thoughts and prayers are with you during this difficult time. I too know the importance of the love and support of a partner in both politics and life. The way Cheryl lived her life is an inspiration to us all and it is my hope that you will continue to find strength and consolation in her memory.

Sincerely,

Jack Layton

Jack Layton MP

On August 22nd, Jack passed away too.

His final letter to Canadians was phenomenal. In Edmonton, an amazing memorial was held with thousands of people in Edmonton. It was an amazing tribute to a great man. It reminded me of the same simultaneous outpouring of grief and love that I had witnessed when Grant passed away.

I now had to decide what to do with myself without Cheryl. Sitting around our condo in Edmonton or Mazatlán wouldn't be healthy. I needed to keep busy.

Through all of the grief of the summer, I had a seat on the Candidate Search Committee for the Alberta NDP, as it geared up for an election either in the fall or spring. I hadn't been paying much attention to provincial politics throughout 2011, but I'm always happy to make calls to encourage people to run for office.

Stelmach had announced he would resign at the same time as Cheryl had been first diagnosed. He had played the same "Long Goodbye" trick as Ralph Klein. The PCs were deep into a summer leadership race, and I thought Gary Mar was set to be Premier.

We expected that once a new leader was picked, an election would follow in October. From 2008, Brian and Rachel had sat as the lone MLAs, and we badly needed to bring in some new NDP MLAs. Overall, candidate search had gone well, with one notable exception.

Edmonton Glenora is a set of neighbourhoods just west of Edmonton's downtown. Parts of it are affluent "old money" neighbourhoods (like Rosedale in Toronto or Mount Royal in Montreal), and working family neighbourhoods, just south of the Yellowhead expressway. It was pretty far from the neighbourhoods where I had run previously. We'd never had much success there, with the exception of 2004, when former ATA President Larry Booi almost won it.

It occurred to me that maybe this was a hole I needed to fill. There was a lot of potential for the NDP there, and the people of Glenora deserved a committed NDP candidate, ready to challenge the PCs. I now found myself with a lot of time on my hands.

My family thought it'd be a good idea. I went for a beer with Brian Mason and Rachel Notley. They were understandably concerned at first. Brian asked "Are you sure you want to do this?" with a hint of concern.

I was. I needed to move on from Cheryl's death, the NDP members in Glenora felt it would be helpful, and Edmonton Glenora needed someone to challenge the PCs.

One of the bonuses was that I got to work with an old friend on the campaign. Alex McEachern was now the riding association president for

Edmonton Glenora, and he was pretty excited to have me on board. In fact, I thought he seemed reinvigorated by it.

Alison Redford proved to be the third Leadership upset in a row. She didn't call the snap election in October that we feared, so I had some time to knock on doors and plan a good nomination meeting. I started with those "Old Money" neighbourhoods along Edmonton's River Valley just to get a sense of what I was up against.

It was a very different experience compared to my familiar neighbourhoods of Alberta Avenue or Beverly or Riverdale. I was surprised about two things: these rich families were actually happy to see their New Democrat candidate, and twenty years after losing the job, they still remembered me from being Leader of the Opposition.

The Liberals, who had won the riding in 2004, tried to kick up a fuss that I was a "carpetbagger" and that it was somehow immoral to run in a riding I didn't live in. I can tell you this: after knocking on a few thousand doors, no one in Glenora seemed to care.

Another surprise was that Glenorans didn't seem to know who their PC MLA was. It might be understandable that east Edmontonians wouldn't know Peter Goldring, who was a Tory backbencher.

But Heather Klimchuck was a cabinet minister. For all the Tories I ran against, I never had to run against a sitting cabinet minister. I will say this: she did a lot more work to win back her own riding during the campaign than most Tory incumbents I've run against.

I was also running against a deputy leader of sorts. In the years running up to that election, there had been an effort to create an "Alberta Party". To this day, I'm hard pressed to tell you what policies or values they were running on. They seemed to flip-flop on just about every issue. They had made a former school board trustee, Sue Huff, their deputy leader and she was also running in Edmonton Glenora.

If nothing else, they did succeed in driving our NDP volunteers nuts. More than anything else she could have taken a stand on; Huff and her Twitter supporters would complain about me knocking on the doors of "their" supporters.

How naïve is that? When I canvass, I knock on every door. Why would I, or any other self-respecting candidate, skip a door just because another party had a sign on the lawn? Even if they do support another party, a voter deserves to get their knock on the door and have their say.

But if you ask Sue Huff and the Alberta Party folks, apparently this was a great crime against democracy. They didn't talk about much else for the duration of the campaign. For their trouble, they got a whopping 8% of the vote in the riding. I guess the other 92% didn't mind if I visited, regardless of what sign was on the lawn.

The next surprise was all the leaders who visited our riding, especially when you consider it's just one out of 87. Brian Mason came and did a few media events, which went fine. But then Premier Redford would show up the very next day, once in the exact same location we had been in. Then the Liberal leader, Raj Sherman, would crash her event in that very same place.

I guess Redford had good reason to visit so often. About halfway though, I was pretty positive and thought that we might be within striking distance of winning. However, as quickly as that momentum came, it went.

Like flicking a light switch, I started having people tell me that they were terrified of the Wildrose party, whom media were starting to claim were poised to win government, largely on the strength of their popularity in Southern Alberta. They supported me, but they wouldn't vote for me because they somehow felt that the PC government that had been eroding their province for decades was still more palatable than the "extremists" in the Wild Rose.

Regardless of what was going on in Southern Alberta, I knew full well that Don Koziak, the Wildrose candidate (and son of my fraternity brother and fellow MLA, Julian Koziak) wasn't going to win Edmonton Glenora. No matter what I said, I really didn't have a clever answer to calm these people down.

By the time election night came, I was still a little optimistic. I was confident that I had lapped the Liberals and Wild Rose, but I didn't feel that I and other NDP candidates had come up with an answer to Edmonton's panic over the Wildrose. When the result came in, I found I hadn't.

I am convinced that we were set to win Edmonton Glenora, as well as Edmonton Gold Bar and Lethbridge West before that Wildrose panic set in. We had very good showings in all three of those ridings, but not the wins we could have had.

I was happy that David Eggen won back his seat in neighbouring Edmonton Calder, but I was very surprised that his race had only been won by 3%. I felt the same for Deron Bilous, who re-took my old riding of Edmonton Beverly-Clareview, but only by 2%.

Part 8: Winning

When I left the Edmonton Public School Board in 2004 to return to the Legislature, David Colburn had won my seat (Ward D) in the subsequent election. Over the course of three terms, he had been a good trustee in my opinion, and we shared a lot of the same values.

Eight years later, in the fall of 2012, he called me up to let me know that he would be running for city council, instead of re-election as a school board trustee. He suggested to me that I should run in his place and return to the school board in the same ward I had represented previously from 2001 to 2004.

I spent a long winter in Mazatlán thinking about Dave's suggestion. I had a great time away from the pressures of being a candidate after doing that job almost non-stop for four years.

In the back of my head, I kept telling myself: "There's got to be something more than retirement." I still felt motivated and healthy enough to contribute to my community. I just wasn't ready to lay in the sun six months of the year.

When I got back, I chatted with the people whose advice I trusted. Should I do this? What would I propose in a campaign? How much campaign funding did I need and where would it come from? In response, no one tried to talk me out of it, and there was enthusiasm from my friends and previous supporters in Ward D's neighbourhoods.

In the late spring of 2013, I started door-knocking again, and had a good reception. School board elections are fairly tame compared to federal and provincial elections. From June to October, all there was to my campaign was door knocking, a couple of leaflets, and some signs on lawns.

My first run for school board had been dominated by the issue of school closures. But in the previous 2010-2013 term, the school board had reformed the horrible process that had led to so many fights over school closures. By the time I ran in 2013, the issues were more varied. Now, my campaign was discussing replacing old schools with new buildings, especially in the Beverly and Highlands neighbourhoods in my East Edmonton ward.

I hadn't won an election since 2004. After that, I had lost four elections in four years from 2008 through 2012. It felt nice to finally win again with 61%. It felt even better to know what I could do with myself for the next four years.

Compared to the conservative board that was elected in 2001, this board had more of a mix, philosophically. But at the same time, we didn't have big splits or disagreements. This board also all knew they were politicians, not former administrators. This group was far more independent-minded than my first board.

It was also a younger crowd, led by Board Chair Sarah Hoffman, just over 30 years old herself. Sarah had been a researcher with the NDP caucus shortly before my defeat in 2008, and had stayed on with the caucus until 2010, when she won a seat on the school board in Edmonton's southeast end. She had also won battles against school closures and had encouraged me to run in 2013.

Being a school board trustee in 2013 was now a much busier job. I quickly immersed myself in the school visits, meetings, and community events.

Hoffman appointed me chair of the infrastructure committee which dealt with the building of new schools, which was a pleasant change from fighting the destruction of schools. There were days where it got taxing, but I was glad I took on the challenge of public service one last time.

Beverly's and Highlands' schools were aging badly. The public told us clearly in consultation that they wanted their schools replaced. I worked with Deron Bilous, now a NDP cabinet minister, to find the funding and create a plan for a new school.

The new Beverly school would be named after Ivor Dent, a great New Democrat. And he didn't just deserve that honor from his time as Mayor. He had also been a great principle in Rundle Heights, located in east Beverly.

Replacing older inner-city schools wasn't the only issue for me. We had to tackle the sprawling suburbs around Edmonton as well and get new schools there. As I write this, 25% of students live west of the Anthony Henday Parkway, Edmonton's ring road, in brand new subdivisions.

The kids we teach in Edmonton schools are different now as well. We have nearly 100,000 kids to teach. Nearly 10% are English language learners. There's also a growing First Nations population that has its own cultural needs. This was particularly true in my ward and I spent a lot of time working to create schools and school programs that could meet those cultural needs.

In the spring of 2014, Brian Mason resigned the leadership of the Alberta NDP. After ten years as leader and winning ten local election campaigns municipally and provincially, he was ready to step back.

He had talked to me about retirement for some time, but I encouraged him not to rule out running as leader again. I thought Brian had been gaining stature, and maybe should have stayed on.

I was asked to sit on the Leadership contest rules committee, so that immediately meant I wasn't going to endorse anyone. But I paid attention to the race and thought all three candidates did a great job.

There wasn't any of the acrimony that existed in the PC party's recent leadership races and David Eggen, Rod Loyola, and Rachel Notley treated each other with respect. Some claimed this peaceful dialogue was boring, but I thought it was healthy for the party.

Rachel Notley won with 70%, and I wasn't surprised. It was great to see a Notley in leadership again. That day, the activists that crowded around her made me think about the contrast to the 1993 election night, when we lost a generation of great potential MLAs and activists.

The day after she won the leadership was the 30th anniversary of Grant's death. The party held a memorial at the downtown Edmonton park that bears his name. To this day, I think Grant's life proves that you can have an impact against all odds. I also got to tell Rachel how proud both Grant and her mother Sandy would be of her.

Comparatively, 2014 brought turmoil in the PC Party. Premier Alison Redford was burdened with numerous scandals and resigned. She was replaced temporarily with David Hancock, and finally former federal cabinet minister Jim Prentice.

I had thought Jim Prentice was a good choice as leader and premier for the PCs. He had actually been the PC candidate that ran against Bob Hawkesworth in 1986 and lost. But he had subsequently won a federal seat in 2004. He seemed to be a more moderate conservative and had been a relatively successful cabinet minister in the Harper government.

By November of 2014, Brian Mason called me up. He felt that Prentice would be calling a snap election in 2015, and he was leaning towards running again in that election, even if he wasn't a leader anymore.

The next month, Alberta politics got a shock when the Leader of the Opposition, Danielle Smith, left her party to join the Progressive Conservatives and took a pack of MLAs with her. The Wildrose was left with just five seats and seemingly moribund.

My first thought when watching this take place was "There's so much cynicism in politics, this'll just add to it." I don't think there's much ideological difference between the PCs and Wildrose, but to just collapse meant that nobody was served well. In fact, democracy was hurt.

I've got no respect for those people who abandoned their party that easily. People voted these MLAs in to represent a party and expected them to stick to those values for the duration of the term. If you don't think your political career is going the way you want, then resign or sit as an independent.

I've seen every PC victory since 1971 and I thought that a 2015 election would be another inevitable PC victory, just like everyone else. But I also thought that the Wildrose couldn't be used to scare NDP supporters into voting PC, like Alison Redford had done so expertly in 2012. At the beginning of the campaign, I though the NDP could win more seats in Edmonton and Lethbridge, but that was about it.

But soon after Prentice became Premier, oil prices fell. Very quickly, he began ramping up the old PC austerity rhetoric. But he was also making dumb statements, like saying that Albertans needed to "look in the mirror" when deciding who was at fault for the Alberta deficit, and saying that Albertans had "had the best of everything" from government, when they clearly hadn't.

He finished the shortened spring sitting of the Legislature with a budget that stung most Alberta families with cutbacks and new taxes but didn't touch the corporate sector. No one was buying the same austerity rhetoric that had worked so well in 1993. Again, like so many PC Premiers before him, he didn't seriously address the revenue side of the deficit, and just cut services and imposed silly little taxes on families.

Prentice's remarks were reminiscent of Don Getty's problems with communicating and putting his foot in his mouth. And just like Getty in 1989, he called an election a year early.

Even though I'd run in the previous three provincial elections, there was no question of running again. I had my seat on the school board to keep me busy, and I felt like I was finally through with being a candidate. Even with what happened next, I have no regrets about this.

During the election, I used what spare time I had to canvass for Brian Mason and Sarah Hoffman, who had stepped down as school board chair and was running in Edmonton Glenora. By the first week, I knew we were going to win the majority of seats in Edmonton. You could sense the anger at the PCs and the goodwill for our candidates, just like in 1986.

I didn't see the now-infamous 2015 Leaders' Debate. I had a school board meeting that night. But I heard about Jim Prentice making his "Math is Hard" crack at Rachel Notley.

Just like everyone else, I cringed at the condescending tone when I saw the highlights. And Brian Jean wasn't a particularly good debater and was only prepared to repeat a single line on taxes. The media declared Rachel the winner.

In itself, winning a debate doesn't win you an election. I learned that firsthand in 1993 after getting the same kind of praise and then getting shut out.

But that's when we all saw polls that the NDP could be the government of Alberta. It was unthinkable, even to me. I kept knocking on doors for Brian and Sarah, and I wouldn't allow myself to get too wound up. Going into the last days of the election, I thought we could sweep Edmonton and gain enough seats to form a minority government, but I never saw a majority government coming.

A couple of days before Election Day, I got a call from the NDP central campaign. I got asked to be a M.C. for the election night party for all Edmonton New Democrats in the Westin Hotel. Former NDP staffer Michele Jackson and I would go up to the mic and announce every time the NDP won a seat.

The night started off with a brief spell when the PC seemed to lead. That lead would be short-lived. I became very busy that night and started having to announce new NDP MLAs from across the province.

The moment I'll never forget was when I had to announce one of the most improbable wins of the night: Cameron Westhead was the new NDP MLA for Banff-Cochrane. We'd never come close to winning this Southern Alberta seat filled with mountains, cattle ranches, and tourist towns. That was the moment I realized we would have an Alberta NDP government.

The room I was standing in front of was packed with thousands of people. I finished my job around 9:30 PM. As I walked into the giant crowd, I had a lot of people patting me on the back and telling me how important I had been in creating that historical night.

I saw the new Premier of Alberta only briefly that night. We hugged. Once again, I told her that my friends, Grant and Sandy Notley, would have been very proud of her. In fact, I think it would've blown Grant's mind, and I think he would've been proud of what they've done since.

In the days after, I was surprised by getting a lot of media calls, the most I'd gotten since I was a party leader myself. I also got calls for advice from new MLAs.

My first piece of advice to the new MLAs was this: don't get overwhelmed by what goes on in the Legislature and trying to learn all the arcane rules. You can pick up what you need to know as you go along.

Instead, immerse yourself in your riding. Build a well-functioning constituency office and keep canvassing and going to events in your riding. That's where politics really happens. It's where you can listen, change lives, and get re-elected as well.

It isn't easy. This government must balance their beliefs against the fiscal mess that they've inherited. But they're smart people and they'll meet the learning curve. I'm optimistic that they'll overcome these challenges. I'm proud of Rachel and what she's done in the Premier's chair, and I know Grant and Sandy would be even more so.

When my term neared its end, I had no compulsion to run again. A great candidate, Trisha Estabrooks was ready to run in my place. I was happy to endorse her, and happier when she won.

My decision was the result of getting a new job: Chair of the Board of Governors for the Northern Alberta Institute of Technology, or "NAIT", as every Albertan calls it. It's the post-secondary polytechnic college that students go to from all over Northern Alberta. I had met one of the vice-presidents and was surprised to be asked to chair this board. They felt I was qualified based on my 15 years in the Legislature and 7 on a school board.

I was entirely an uncontroversial choice. A Liberal MLA, David Swann, suggested I shouldn't have gotten this spot because of my partisan past. My response was simple: I don't care.

There are twenty board members, mainly people from industry, and we make the broader decisions for the institution. It's a few speeches, a lot of complicated meetings and a lot of reading, but it's great to stay involved in education.

I got to give a tour for Jagmeet Singh, shortly after he became the new Federal NDP Leader. He visited NAIT, and I got to give him an official tour and go for lunch afterwards.

I was about to start talking education when Jagmeet said "Ray, I want to talk about something else." He asked me for my view of the Kinder Morgan pipeline and Rachel's advocacy for that project, considering how controversial it was in B.C.

I'm not sure he liked my answer. "Look, I stand behind Rachel on this," I replied. "It's true that we're moving away from fossil fuels, and we should be doing that. But it's ludicrous that we can just switch off and move to alternative energy overnight."

He wasn't uptight to hear this and we had a good discussion. I think he was just genuinely trying to learn about the views of Alberta New Democrats.

The NDP's provincial election was only one of two life-changing events for me in May of 2015.

Evelyn David was an educational resource developer and artist. She had also been a long-time friend of Cheryl's. As it turned out, she had designed leaflets for the NDP in the 1982 election, including mine.

She had taken a sign and come to an event for my 2013 school board campaign. After I won my school board seat, we went for dinner. As the cliché goes, one thing led to another.

We dated and moved in together in 2014. Shortly before the provincial election we went to visit her family in the Philippines. I met loads of her relatives and I saw Manilla, one of the largest cities in the world.

My enduring memory of Manila is a very simple school visit. It got around to Evelyn's extended family that I was a school board trustee, and this got me an invite to visit a graduation ceremony for Grade Six students. For a lot of the kids, it'd be the only education they'd get, so it was an emotional event for every person in the room.

A couple of weeks after Election Day, Evelyn and I got married in the Riverdale Community League hall, in Edmonton's beautiful river valley. My long-time friend, Brian Mason, officiated.

Surprisingly, I was very nervous on the day. I've married a lot of people, but I'd never had a "normal" wedding before. I didn't want to make an ass of myself. But I love Evelyn and I wanted to go through with a new marriage. And I know Cheryl would have very much approved of her.

What happens next? Whenever I've had to do some serious thinking, I like to go down to Mazatlán and take a walk on the beach. It's a pleasant beach and it's a good place to be calm and think things through, especially what to do next.

I think I'll go for a walk.

Epilogue
By John Ashton

Neither Ray nor I sought the task of crafting these memoirs. We did this because we were being asked to, rather forcefully, by the many people who had worked with him over the years. While Ray is not one to dwell too much on the past, many Albertans felt that his experiences were too valuable to lose to time. Having a bit of training in writing from university, this "campaign manager" was effectively assigned to seeing it done.

Ray found working on this book to be an irritation and distraction, albeit an unavoidable one. He frequently referred to the many hours of interviews required for the composition as "torture sessions."

About halfway through the interview process that Ray disliked so much, I took a shot at trying to make the process less onerous for both of us.

Ray and I are both fans of Edmonton Eskimos football. I had two tickets for a sunny Saturday afternoon game against the Winnipeg Blue Bombers and I thought we'd do a round of interviews over a pint or two and then take in the game.

We were walking into Commonwealth Stadium when a young woman strode by us, wearing an Eskimos jersey with the name and number of the legendary hard-hitting linebacker, Danny Kepley. This woman was clearly in her early twenties, far too young to have remembered Kepley winning six Grey Cups, as Ray had watched in the 1970s and 80s.

Ray pointed her out. "Why is she wearing that jersey?" he asked, rhetorically. "Danny Kepley's from my generation, not hers. You would think she'd get a jersey with a player from today."

I thought about it a second. "That's true." I replied. "But at the same time, Danny Kepley's a legend. He's not just special to your generation. He belongs to the ages now." Ray shrugged, and we got in line to get into the stadium.

As I think about my last eleven years working with Ray, and Ray's supporters, I see parallels between him and Danny Kepley.

The people who worked on Ray's elections in 2008 and 2011 were much younger than Ray. If you had walked into his campaign offices, you would have seen a lot of people in their twenties and thirties. These people (including myself) are too young to remember Ray as a leader of the

Alberta NDP and the Official Opposition. Some hadn't even been born in 1993 when Ray relinquished his leadership.

This came as a surprise to me, even as I was managing that 2011 campaign. Why were people, some forty years younger than Ray, there? Why were they spending their own time making phone calls and knocking on doors?

I've come to believe that it's the same reason that a young woman would be a fan of a football player who retired ten years before she was born. Because the impact of what was achieved and what it represents can't be limited to a generation.

Ray is a person who was born and raised in a quintessential rural Albertan childhood. He lived in both of our province's major cities. He is as Albertan as steak and rodeo. And he led a political party like an Albertan, running on progressive values and personal integrity, articulated in simple terms, rather than academic arguments or Machiavellian scheming.

He didn't win government as his BC and Saskatchewan contemporaries did, or as Rachel Notley would go on to do. But he did prove that more than a quarter of a million Albertans could be convinced to vote for egalitarianism over unfettered capitalism and did it twice.

I believe that young Albertans who kick against the conservative orthodoxy inflicted on them look to Ray with hope that his mark can be achieved again, and surpassed. They may not have been there for that fervently optimistic night in 1986, but they knew that if he can reach that pinnacle, so can they. That's why you could still find them campaigning for the man a quarter of a century later.

When he showed up in my office for another "torture session", the first thing he would talk about is the school visits he does as a school board trustee. While there was no requirement for Ray to do these visits, he routinely showed up at schools to meet with principals, teachers, parents, and the children in his ward. He is still having an impact on those schools and the lives of Albertan children. He's as active and enthusiastic an advocate for his values as ever.

That means there's at least one more generation of Ray Martin supporters to come. And that means if you walk into a NDP campaign office years from now, you may see a young Albertan with a NDP shirt with Ray's name on it.